Organizing Residential Utilities: A New Approach to Housing Quality

U.S. Dept of Housing and Urban
Development, et al., Kent Larson

Organizing Residential Utilities: A New Approach to Housing Quality

Organizing Residential Utilities:
A New Approach to Housing Quality

Prepared for:

U.S. Department of Housing and Urban
Development
Office of Policy Development and Research
Washington, DC

Prepared by:

Richard Topping
Tyson Lawrence
Justin Spencer
TIAX LLC
Cambridge, Massachusetts

and

Kent Larson
TJ McLeish
The House_n Research Group
Massachusetts Institute of Technology
Cambridge, Massachusetts

November 2004

Acknowledgements

The authors would like to recognize the advisory team, which helped contribute to the industry background and provided review of concepts. The advisory team included Tedd Benson, Bensonwood Homes; Ray Cudwadie, Deluxe Homes; Al Marzullo, TKG East Engineering; John Tocci, Tocci Building; Nelson Oliveira, Nelson Group Construction; Ling Yi Liu, Oak Tree Development; Jim Petersen, Pulte Home Sciences; Randy Luther, Centex Homes; Hiroshi Abe, Seki Sui Homes; Ari Griffner, Griffner-Haus; and John Benson, Meadwestvaco. Thanks also to Christine Murner, GE Plastics, for providing a tour of the Living Environments House. The authors would also like to thank David Dacquisto, Newport Partners; Mark Nowak, Newport Partners; Michael Crosbie, Ph.D., RA, Steven Winter Associates; and Ron Wakefield, Ph.D., Virginia Tech, for providing review and discussion via teleconference during the literature review.

The authors gratefully acknowledge the help and guidance provided by Mike Blanford and Luis Borray from HUD.

Disclaimer

Table of Contents

List of Exhibits

1 Summary

1.1 Background

Utility systems are everywhere in the home. What were once major innovations – central heating, hot and cold running water, and electric lights – have become so commonplace as to be taken for granted. In fact, the network of utilities (pipes, wires, and ducts) in the home is now relatively simple compared to those in some of the other environments that people occupy – airplanes, ships, cars, etc. Although the systems in the home are comparatively uncomplicated, their installation involves inefficient, labor-intensive processes that would not be tolerated in other products and industries, such as those mentioned above. Utilities are run almost haphazardly through the walls of stick-built homes, sometimes compromising structure and insulating integrity, and always making repair and modification difficult. In the future, utilities will inevitably become more complicated as homes become centers of work, learning, communication, entertainment, preventative health care, and distributed energy production. The new utility systems that emerge to meet these functions will likely include advanced control systems, LED or fiber-optic lighting, wireless and wired data networks, additional fire safety plumbing, building-integrated photovoltaics, and ubiquitous low-cost sensors for security, health, comfort, etc. Existing utility systems can also be expected to expand. Conventional entangled processes will increase the complexity and cost of construction, and could inhibit the introduction of new utility systems. Furthermore, new building technologies and construction techniques have the potential to compound the problem: utility entanglement could become a major roadblock to innovation in home construction.

1.2 Definition of Terms

How to disentangle utilities and when it is economically beneficial to do so are complex questions that must factor in the technologies used in both the utility systems and the structure, the business model of the builder (site-based or factory-based, custom or generic), and the surrounding industry environment (codes, standards, contracting systems, specialization, etc.). The following key terms will be defined as follows for the purposes of this report:

Utilities: The distribution systems for electricity, data, plumbing, heating, ventilation, and air conditioning (HVAC), and gas within single-family homes.

Entangled Utilities: Pipes, ducts, and wires that are embedded in walls, floors, and ceilings without predefined accessible pathways.

Disentangling Utilities: Organizing utilities and increasing the efficiency of utility installation (and repair and renovation) by separating and decoupling pipes, ducts, and wires from the structure and finish, and by creating dedicated accessible pathways.

Innovation: Ideas, technologies, and methods that are new to the building industry.

Site-based: Most of the construction takes place in the location in which the final structure will stand.

Factory-based: A majority of the construction takes place in one or more factory locations where components are manufactured for final assembly on site.

Custom: Unique homes that have been tailored to the specific needs of a single homebuyer.

Generic: Repetitive homes that allow only minor cosmetic changes from one buyer to the next, such as countertop selection, or specific choices, such as creating two small bedrooms or one large bedroom from the same space.

Codes: A systematic collection of regulations and rules of building procedure enforced by government inspectors.

Standards: Specifications for sizes and practices that are widely recognized or employed, such as the RJ-45 plug used for Cat-5 data wiring.

1.3 Problem Definition

Embedding pipes, ducts, and wires in walls, floors, and ceilings haphazardly without planning or dedicated spaces can increase cost during initial construction, especially in the case of custom factory-based systems. Once a home is built, entangled utilities are difficult to modify, because they are embedded in the structure and hidden behind drywall. Unfortunately, access to utilities almost always becomes necessary at some point due to remodeling or other changes, for example, adding data wiring or repairing household plumbing.

Entangled utilities can:
- Lead to inefficiency in initial construction
- Compromise structural integrity
- Negatively affect utility function
- Negatively impact sound and heat insulation function
- Obstruct rework, renovation, and repair

1.4 Objective

This report is designed to outline methods of disentangling utilities, with the goal of increasing the functionality of housing, while simultaneously reducing its cost. Disentangling of utilities should have the following positive impacts:
- Reduce cost of utility installation
- Simplify the home construction process, resulting in less rework
- Reduce time of construction
- Reduce home maintenance costs
- Reduce cost of renovations

- Reduce cost of customization in initial build and renovation
- Enable increased homeowner participation in home alterations

1.5 Synopsis of Findings

Providing designated, decoupled, and accessible space for utilities can reduce cost and time during initial construction, particularly, for factory-based custom builders. It can also allow utility systems to be modified or repaired over time without performing major demolition and reconstruction. While not technically disentangling, flexible utilities with faster connections can ease installation and subsequent alteration and are included as related topics. Some products exist today that can help alleviate entanglement (for example raceways and open web floor trusses), but implementing disentanglement innovations involves risk and cost. Decoupling utilities from the structure and finish requires redesign of structural systems, which could lead to increased material costs and fundamental changes to the way most contractors install utilities. This, in turn, would require training. Providing accessibility requires new finish materials and methods that are typically more expensive than drywall. These changes and the training required represent risk for a builder who has already optimized his system. Making changes to coordination methods, structural systems, and finish materials all have the potential to increase cost. The benefits of disentanglement must be weighed against these associated costs and risks.

Market penetration of disentangling technologies has been limited due to various factors that make the profitability of disentanglement difficult for most builders to realize. These factors include:

- Inability to market disentanglement as a major benefit to the average consumer.
- A lack of vertical integration to allow the potential cost savings of disentanglement to be captured by those who must take the risk.
- A short-term contracting system that rewards predictability and "tried and true" methods, rather than major method changes that might be beneficial in the long term.
- The fragmented and regional nature of small builders limits the economies of scale that can be achieved by using manufactured components that can more easily integrate disentangling features.
- Changes to the national model codes are generally too slow and expensive for builders or manufacturers to pursue unless they have capital and can anticipate high sales volume in the short term, which may not be realistic for some disentangling methods or technologies.
- Building codes adopted and interpreted on a local basis can limit the application of products and methods, whether national certification is obtained or not.
- Inability to achieve proper compensation for disentanglement innovations that add value over the long life of the building.

Custom factory-based construction methods overcome some of these factors and stand to benefit the most from disentanglement. Therefore, these methods provide the greatest opportunity in the near term for capturing value from disentanglement during initial construction. Use of interchangeable housing parts with standardized connections to achieve optimized solutions tailored to each homebuyer has great potential as a future method of residential construction. The off-site prefabrication of components in a controlled environment with a team-oriented workforce can reduce the costs associated with time-gating (waiting for one subcontractor to finish before another can start), contracting, and rework. Disentanglement will be crucial to this method, because of the complex interactions between components and the preplanned nature of the building process. For example, a plumber would no longer be able to drill or cut the finished structure to make space for pipes. Specific spaces must be allocated ahead of time, because of the tightly engineered and optimized nature of the system. Disentanglement can also be more easily implemented in this environment, because the builder has integrated the process and therefore can directly control the training of his workers and reap the benefit of the gains in efficiency over time. If the work were subcontracted on a case-by-case basis, the builder would take a great risk by incurring the expense necessary to teach subcontractors the new method. Customization with a component-based system requires disentanglement to be efficient (high benefit). The vertically integrated nature of factory-based systems and the long-term employment of utility installers allow innovations to be implemented with greater control (lower cost and risk).

Disentangling innovations should be implemented first in high-end housing, because high-end builders tend to have higher margins (more money available for innovation), and a greater ability to differentiate themselves based on this type of innovation. High-end buyers are more likely to be willing to pay more for innovative systems than low-end consumers. Furthermore, innovations generally trickle down more easily than up. Innovations made in low-end housing may not be adopted by mainstream builders, because they are perceived as substandard products or methods simply because they are used in low-end housing. However, if those same innovations are used in high-end construction, the perceived benefit of quality by association – in addition to any potential efficiency benefits – may encourage adoption. Many disentangling innovations may eventually find their way into all housing, but it is prudent to focus initial efforts on the areas that stand to benefit the most with the least upfront cost and risk.

Two examples of high-end custom builders using factory-based manufacturing systems are Bensonwood Homes of New Hampshire and Griffnerhaus of Austria. The potential for reduction in the cost of customization drives these builders to look at methods of disentangling utility systems. Major barriers they identified as inhibiting mass customization today are building regulations and the limited availability of components with standardized connections. The formation of industry working groups to develop standard specifications for connections and to educate code-forming bodies on the barriers in the model code would enable more manufacturers to enter the high-value component market. This would increase the variety of available components and reduce their cost. On a local basis, a searchable national database of local variances granted could allow localities to more easily accept innovations that had been approved in another locality, but had not yet been incorporated into the model code. Another possible change to the code system that could help factory-based builders would be to adjust the inspection system. Rather than forcing a factory-based builder to deal with a new inspector in each locality, a single inspector could be assigned to the factory for each state in which that factory ships homes, allowing the builder to develop trust with the inspector, much as a local subcontractor does. The success of this building system would in turn allow for greater disentanglement, because this type of factory-based custom builder is the most likely to capture the value of disentanglement during initial construction.

Value from the disentanglement of utilities also accrues after initial construction. Renovation and repair of utilities is much easier when they are initially disentangled. This benefit generally accrues to the second buyer of the home, who decides to renovate after moving in. Few new homebuyers live in their homes long enough to adequately capture this value for themselves, and realtors, lenders, and existing home buyers have little means for promoting the value of disentanglement. Criteria for evaluating the degree to which homes have been built to allow for change over time could assist in the capture of this value, increasing the resale value of homes with disentangled utilities. This could be modeled on the successful LEED program, which has greatly increased awareness of environmental concerns within the construction industry. Government or lender incentives based on the increased lifetime value of the home could further increase the advantage to builders adopting disentangling innovations.

It is important to gain a good understanding of how the value of disentanglement can be captured and which areas of the industry would most readily adopt disentangling ideas. However, there are also many specific recommendations for how to best separate and decouple the pipes, ducts, and wires from structure and finish; create predefined, accessible pathways; and, generally, increase the organization of utilities.

They include:
- Using software and digital libraries of building components to allow efficient and accurate planning to predefine utility pathways before construction begins.
- Separating building layers by lifespan, decoupling utilities from structure with open web floor trusses and raceways, and providing for access.
- Creating an integrated utility gateway that brings all of the services into the home in a single location.
- Creating integrated utility modules, for example a fully plumbed bathroom wall, which can be manufactured as one piece in a factory in a disentangled manner.
- Increasing the use of quick connect electrical and plumbing components to allow even greater gains in efficiency and ease of renovation from disentangling.
- Anticipating potential future utility systems before they are widely implemented and making allowances for their eventual installation.
- Working with the HVAC industry to create a distributed modular system that limits distribution requirements and reduces entanglement.
- Creating a single shared low-bandwidth data network to replace proprietary lighting control, HVAC control, security, and sensor networks.

In the final analysis, disentanglement of utilities has the most potential benefit for the housing industry when used with certain building systems. Some innovations like raceways, floor trusses, and flexible service connections have already been developed, but have experienced limited market penetration due to several factors examined in this report. Collaboration among HUD and industry working groups, including builders and housing researchers, to design, test, and evaluate these concepts could be an effective next step in enabling disentanglement.

2   Review of Entanglement

Information was collected from a wide variety of sources to understand how residential utility systems are currently entangled, how they became that way, and what efforts have been undertaken to solve these problems in the United States and internationally.

2.1   The Development of Entanglement Over Time

A study of the history of home utilities in America reveals a repeating pattern of major utility technology development, followed by widespread retrofitting of existing homes and incorporation of the technology into new homes. Meanwhile, the structural system used for the majority of homes remained relatively constant. In the 1800s, most homes were simple structures with the only one utility system, a fireplace or stove and accompanying chimney, typically in the center of the home. This was where cooking was performed and heat provided. To heat additional rooms, generally more chimneys and fireplaces were added. Early American homeowners often built the house by themselves with help from others. Balloon framing came into use during the early to mid-1800s with its "stick built" stud walls.[1]

In the late 1800s and early 1900s, the addition of utility systems was quite rapid. First, running water was introduced, followed quickly by gas for lighting, cooking, and heating, full indoor plumbing and hot water, electricity for lighting and appliances, and residential telephones. In the latter half of the 1900s, central air-conditioning became prevalent, with its requirements for large ducts to distribute conditioned air through the home. Additional data systems (generally for security and the Internet) have become standard in many homes during the last decade (see Figure 1).

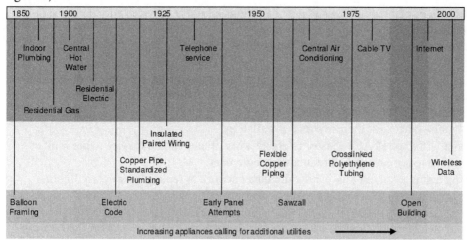

The top row of events tracks the addition of major utility systems into the average home. The second row highlights some important modifications to those basic utilities. The third row indicates the development of key surrounding technologies and ideas.
Figure 1: Utilities Timeline

---

[1] John A. Kouwenhoven. *Made in America: The Arts in Modern Civilization*. New York. 1962.

As utilities became more available and desired, they were simply added into new home designs wherever they could be fit with little regard for integration or system design. This was possibly due to the large amount of empty space available in the walls of a stud-framed home and the ability of contractors to drill through the existing structure to enable passage. Over time, utilities have become more widespread in homes, both in the total number of utility systems and in the distribution of each system. The number of utility systems continues to increase as new systems become available, and it is difficult to predict what new utilities may be necessary in the future. The distribution of utilities has also expanded to meet an increased number of appliances and devices using each utility. Originally there might have been only one or two electrical outlets in a room or in the whole house. Today building codes require that outlets be placed at least once every twelve feet and one on every discontinuous section of wall. Yet, in today's typical home, there is generally only one data (phone, TV cable, Ethernet) outlet per room, sometimes only one per house in older homes. A similar proliferation of these types of outlets may be required in the future.

Over time, homeowners have become less involved in the building process, with the vast majority of homes in postwar suburban America designed and built by professional builders. This has changed the home-building industry from a custom craft, where many homeowners were intimately involved and were making building process innovations to match their personal needs and available resources, to a craft process without customization[2] that builds larger homes with increased functionality at a reduced cost, but with less user participation and satisfaction.

During the rapid expansion of utility systems, the structure of the home has changed very little, except for an increase in the overall size (see Figure 2). By and large, the structural elements have remained the same. Homes are stick-built on-site, in much the same process used in the early 20th century. The combination of a fixed amount of space within the walls, the expansion of utilities, and the increase in insulation has, creating a crowded and entangled situation. The result is a building system that does not maximize "whole house" efficiency.

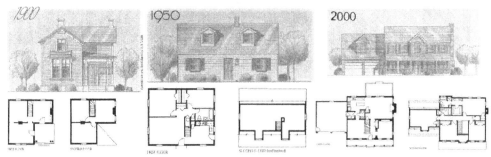

Over the last century, homes have become much larger and more complex, including a greater distribution and variety of utilities (illustrations and floor plans by Rick Vitullo).[3]
Figure 2: Structural and Utility Changes

[2] James Barlow. From craft production to mass customisation. Innovation requirements for the UK housebuilding industry. Housing Studies, 14, 1, 23-42, 1999.
[3] A Century of progress: American Housing 1900-2000, NAHB, 2003.

2.2   Efforts at Disentangling Past and Present

Historically, there have been many attempts at systems-based or "whole house" approaches that, as part of efforts to implement better methods of building, included technologies and processes to deal with the increasing entangling of utilities. Some of the more recent "whole house" efforts addressing disentangling have taken place in Europe and Asia. In the United States, the industry has adapted to the disentanglement of utilities problem by developing a fairly strict order of construction operations and by generally limiting technology changes to individual utility systems. Also, new communication methods, such as cell phones, for quick and easy communication with workers on-site have helped reduce some of the problems resulting from entanglement.

2.2.1   Selected Historical Whole House Efforts

The building industry has made attempts to take a system-wide view of the home. This has often been the result of a change in the structural system. In this type of "whole-house" redesign, designers have repeatedly considered the impacts of utilities. In the nineteenth century, some homes were designed around a central core where all of the utilities were located. Putting in utilities was costly, so they were typically only brought to one or a few locations. Designs worked outward from a large masonry chimney, where heat for room heating and cooking was provided. When water was added, it also was first brought only to this central space, mostly for cooking.[4] The Katherine Beecher House published in "The American Woman's Home" in 1869 is an example of this sort of centralized design, (see Figure 3).[5] Through an efficient centralized design the distribution of utilities is limited and thus the impact on the structure and finish of the house is minimized.

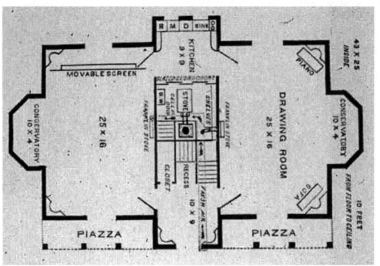

Figure 3: Katherine Beecher House

---

[4] John A. Kouwenhoven. *Made in America: The Arts in Modern Civilization.* New York. 1962
[5] Beecher and Stowe, *The American Woman's Home*, New York, 1869

Another example of disentangling with a central core of utilities is the Dymaxion House (see Figure 4). Buckminster Fuller's effort included a central core of utilities and a radial design that minimized distribution requirements. In addition, the circular shape minimized the exposed exterior surface and a reflective roof reduced heating and cooling loads, resulting in a smaller HVAC system. These advances were accompanied by employing moveable shelves and air vents at the base of walls to help reduce dust accumulation. Despite all this, Fuller's manufactured home design was unsuccessful. It offered no possibility for owners to choose the aesthetic or options they found appealing. Instead, it demanded that they conform to Fuller's radical concepts and look. Few of his advances have been successfully transferred to traditional homes, because his design was very integrated and rigid. It did not allow for useful components to be reused in other home designs. As a result it was not cost effective for other homebuilders to incorporate parts of his system or attempt to build houses similar to the Dymaxion House.

Figure 4: Dymaxion House

The Monsanto Disneyland Home of the Future (see Figure 5) of 1957 also adopted a circular shape with a central core of utilities and radial distribution. It employed plastic walls with high insulation values, which again minimized the HVAC requirements.

Figure 5: Monsanto Disney Land Home of the Future

2.2.2 Open Building Concept

A more flexible approach to whole house design is called open building. The concept of open building is partially embodied by some builders in Europe, such as Grifnerhaus, and a limited number of builders in the United States, such as Bensonwood. The central tenet of this building philosophy involves separating the individual building systems and allowing them to interact in standard ways which permit the systems to be mixed and matched efficiently, and replaced or reconfigured by future occupants to match their individual needs.[6] Figure 6 shows this separation of systems and the frequency with which each system is typically changed.

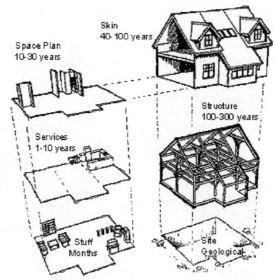

Figure 6: Layers in Open Building from www.bensonwood.com

Most builders pursuing open building try to achieve a cost-effective solution that allows for enough variation to provide individualization. An added benefit is the ease with which the home can be adapted as the occupants or their needs change. The concepts of open building include disentangled utilities. Separating utilities from each other and the structure is part of the separation of layers that is central to this system. This decoupling allows for changes to the utility systems without negatively affecting other parts of the building. Currently, these efforts are in the early stages and have not made significant inroads within the building industry. As a result, the market for manufactured components that could help facilitate disentangling utilities in this manner is limited. The availability of inexpensive advanced components is crucial to the long-term opportunity for cost improvements in open buildings. If the builder must produce all the components for open building in-house, much of the potential financial benefit of the system is lost. The wide success of the open building system will rely on the availability of a variety of interchangeable home components, and this variety has been slow in coming. The open building community is experiencing something of a chicken and egg dilemma. The component manufacturers need a larger market, and a large market requires a greater variety of components.

---

[6] Habraken, N.J., Variations, the Systematic Design of Supports. With J. T. Boekholt, A.P. Thyssen, P.J.M. Dinjens: MIT Laboratory for Architecture and Planning; distributed by the MIT Press, Cambridge, USA and London, 1976.

2.2.3   Disentangling Utilities in Europe and Asia

While the building industry faces different challenges and expectations around the globe, some of the problems and solutions regarding disentangling utilities in Europe and Asia are analogous to those facing builders in the United States. There are homebuilders in Europe, including Griffnerhaus in Austria, that are looking at innovative solutions that may affect disentangling. Different standards and systems, such as building with concrete rather than wood framing and a push to look for new process innovations, have led to some interesting solutions. Griffnerhaus has developed a new panelized wood system that will be largely factory built with a good number of the utilities designed and pre-installed in the walls at the factory. Other component-based systems have been developed as well, including vertical utility cores. The market for innovative utilities solutions has spawned quick-connecting piping and wiring systems intended to shorten on-site construction time for panelized systems. Seki-Sui in Japan has also developed panelized systems that are largely constructed off-site, and some similar innovations to Griffnerhaus to help optimize its panelized method.

In Britain, the government has recently taken an active role in improving the quality of single-family housing. The British building industry may have faced even more criticism than its American counterpart, including assertions that it was stodgy, that its products had durability and quality problems, and that, unlike other industries, it had failed to make efficiency improvements. In short, it was perceived as an industry that hadn't seen any cost and quality improvements in decades. The British set about solving the problems of low-quality housing, starting with the government sponsored Egan report,[7] which set concrete goals for improvements in the housing industry. The industry responded with experiments in housing quality improvement. The INTEGER Consortium focuses on intelligent, green building and includes consideration of disentangling. The Millennium House showcased all of the best quality, environment friendly, flexible, and functional building components that could be assembled, regardless of cost. The intention was to provide a backdrop of what is possible. Included were various disentangling solutions: baseboard and ceiling level in-wall raceways, passive stack ventilation, bathroom pods, wireless data, and open truss floor systems.[8]

The next step in the British improvement process was for various teams, generally consisting of INTEGER, a builder, and a housing provider, to build new housing that followed the INTEGER design philosophy and incorporated the elements of the Millennium home that made sense for the particular building project.[9] Data has been collected from the occupants of these new homes concerning what they like and dislike about their homes. One key aspect of the changing British building philosophy is the emphasis on durability and lifetime utility. Effort is made to allow homes to change over time, as the needs of the occupants change, and to consider the needs of future occupants. With this goal in mind, disentanglement becomes an important feature to allow easier repair, renovation, and addition to different parts of the home.

---

[7] Sir John Egan, Rethinking Construction, report of the Construction Task Force to the Deputy Prime Minister of the UK, John Prescott, 1998.

[8] Building Homes the Integer Way, Building Homes, London, May 2000.

[9] Tomorrow's Housing Today: Good Practice Guide, INTEGER, 2001.

2.2.4   The U.S. Process to Manage Entanglement

Over time, the labor used to build homes has become increasingly specialized. To deal with this specialization and the increasing quantity of utilities that must be installed in the typical home, an order of operations in installing utilities has been developed.

The general order of operations is structure, then utilities, and then finishes. The utilities are generally installed in order from the least flexible to the most.

- HVAC is the first to go in, because it requires the most space and is the most difficult to route around other systems.
- Plumbing and gas are next and must be installed to avoid the HVAC, often resulting in complicated bending paths, and runs of greater length than would be necessary if more organization and integrated planning were employed.
- Electrical wiring, the most ubiquitous of the systems, is installed next.
- Data, the most flexible and smallest system, is generally installed last.

Initially, this order posed little problem in stick-built homes, as there were few utilities, and plenty of room for them to be installed. Over time, as the walls have become more crowded, the various installations have repeatedly run up against each other and the structure. Generally, each type of utility has its own installer, who tries to finish a job in a continuous fashion, remaining on-site for as few days as possible. Each installer generally plans his own project, with some constraints from the house's initial design plans. The initial plans may include the end points of major systems, but often do not specify all end points and rarely specify pathways. Most installer's work is unplanned based on the limited information in the plans and their own expertise. If they create drawings at all, they are generally low quality. There is an emphasis on individual speed and lowest cost by each installer; the installer generally focuses on his own role, rather than thinking about the overall structure of the home. This specialization has become necessary due to the increasing complexity of each utility system and the building codes and inspection processes surrounding each system. Unfortunately, the emphasis on specialization has decreased coordination and increased overall construction time due to time gating, in which one contractor refuses to come to the building site until the previous subcontractor is completely finished. Time gating can result in delays between each utility installation during which no one is even on the job site. In a typical house construction,"30 to 40 individual subcontractors must be coordinated to perform 100 to 150 separate activities."[10] As the overall system becomes more complex, the decisions of one installer have an increasing impact on the overall design, by placing additional constraints on the installation of later systems. This sequential utilities installation approach results, at a minimum, in compromised solutions and sometimes in less than optimal solutions.

2.2.5   Technology Improvements in the U.S.

The ongoing separation and specialization of utility subcontractors have resulted in few disentangling innovations, which are mostly confined to a particular utility subsystems. Some of these innovations consist of larger component blocks (pre-plumbed sinks, toilets, outlets). Others consist of making utility installation more flexible (flexible gas piping, Romex wiring,

---

[10] Walsh, Kenneth D., Anil Sawhney and Howard H. Bashford. *Cycle-time contributions of hyper specialization and time-gating strategies in US residential construction.* 2003.

flexible water piping). These improvements have led to lower cost and higher reliability, but their full potential has not been realized due to a lack of coordination. However, they do provide an avenue of opportunity for building whole-house disentangling solutions.

Some manufacturing standardization within utility subsystems has allowed increased efficiency within each subsystem. At one time, there were no standard increments for pipe diameters, wire gauge, fittings, and duct sizes. Standardization is especially important at connection points. By utilizing standardized connections, components from different manufacturers can be interchanged. With standardization, future replacement of equipment is possible even if the original components are no longer available. Currently, utility systems are standardized at a very basic level. For example, ducts are commonly available in 1" or 2" increments, making it easier to find a size that matches what is currently installed or will interface with products from other companies, such as diffusers, fans, or dampers. Similarly, wire gauges and pipe diameters are standardized to allow for interchangeability between manufacturers and fittings. Higher levels of standardization and standardization that crosses system boundaries without unduly limiting designer or consumer options could be beneficial. This will be discussed further in later sections.

2.2.6 Communication Tools to Aid Disentangling
Recent developments with great potential to empower builders to disentangle utilities include the increased use of communications and the use of automated design technology. CAD systems allow accurate and detailed documentation to be developed quickly. This becomes even more efficient when significant pieces of design are reused whenever possible. Bensonwood Homes in New Hampshire uses this concept extensively, often reusing entire rooms and architectural details in otherwise custom designs. Cell phones, web logs, and e-mail also allow faster and more complete communication among the various stakeholders in producing a home.

2.2.7 Database of Technologies and Components for Disentangling Utilities
A database of potentially relevant disentangling technologies identified in the literature search is indexed in Appendix B. Each entry is categorized and described, including companies that are currently producing each product. Figure 7 shows pictures of a few of the technologies on the list.

From left to right then top to bottom: wire routing aides, baseboard raceways for initial construction and retrofit, tubular skylights, open web floor truss combining wood and steel, all steel truss, and all wood truss. Photos from International Builders Show.

Figure 7: Important Technologies

2.3 The Current State of Utility Systems

The technologies for disentangling utilities currently available represent an opportunity, but not a complete solution. Most of the available technologies and concepts have not been effectively incorporated into building methods, and the status quo remains similar to what is described in Section 2.1, with utilities simply being added wherever they fit. As a result the current state of utilities is a complicated and interwoven jumble, (see Figure 8). All of the systems are entangled in each other, and they are typically difficult to modify or repair. Due to conflicts and interactions among systems, installation is not merely inefficient and labor intensive, it can results in such a haphazard solution that the integrity of utility systems and even the structure is compromised. In order to remedy this physical situation, it is important to have a clear idea of the systems that are involved: structure, electric, data, plumbing, HVAC, and gas. The following sections describe each of these systems in more detail.

Utilities are squeezed in and drilled through in a disorganized way leading to conflicts, inefficiencies, and potential degradation of structure and utilities. Photos from some typical construction situations.
Figure 8: Entanglement Examples

2.3.1 Structure

The most important system in the home, and the most critical one in examining entanglement, is the structure itself. Most single-family homes built in the United States continue to use solid wood platform frames. However, a variety of alternative structural products and techniques are beginning to receive growing acceptance in the marketplace. These range from slight modifications on the stud frame concept to completely new systems. Modifications to the traditional system include engineered wood products, such as I-beam floor joists, panelized walls, and new systems mixed with traditional platform framing. New systems include insulated concrete forms (ICFs), structural insulated panels (SIPs), and light-gauge steel. Because the structure interacts with all the utility systems and because new systems are becoming popular, it is important to be aware of the market penetration of each technology. The following table describes the extent to which builders have adopted four of these methods using the percentage of annual starts with each.

Product Used	Percent of Annual Starts
Insulated Concrete Forms	7.2%
Structural Insulated Panels	8.7%
Light-Gauge Steel Walls	14.9%
Panelized Walls	49.9%

Table 1: Usage of New Structural Technologies
Note: Panelized walls are typical stud-framed walls built in advance.
Source: 2001 *Annual Builder Practices Survey*. Special Tabulation

The ways that utilities are run through these different structural systems varies greatly according to their fundamental differences. The traditional method of removing material from the structure as needed to create runs for utilities continues to be applied for engineered wood products like I-beam floor joists. Simply drilling holes is used to some extent in concrete, SIPs, and steel, but it is much more difficult[11] and has forced builders to develop new methods of running utilities and to more carefully plan distribution paths before the structure is assembled. Raceways and conduit are embedded in concrete where wires will be run. Space for wires and plumbing are routed out of the insulation in SIPs in the factory during the manufacturing of panels.[12] Steel framing is often manufactured with precut holes to allow for utility runs[13] (see Figure 9).

---

[11] Nelson Oliveira, Nelson Group Construction, personal interview, December 2003.

[12] PaceMaker product literature.

[13] FrameMax product literature.

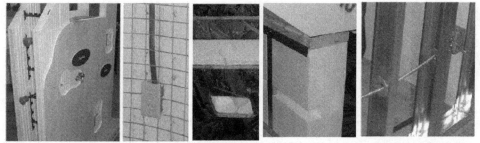

From left to right: Insulated concrete forms with utilities run through spaces routed out of the Styrofoam, insulated spray-on concrete form with conduit run before spraying, SIPS with factory created conduit in insulation, new SIPS with factory created raceway, and steel framing with plastic bushings. Photos from International Builders Show.
Figure 9: Routing of Utilities Through Different Structural Systems

2.3.2 Electricity Distribution
The configuration of the utilities themselves is also important to disentanglement. In most cases, electricity is carried throughout the home by copper Romex cable. This cable is run from a central breaker box in separate circuits to provide power to outlets, appliances, and lights. Hard-wired switches that physically break the circuit to prevent power from continuing to the light fixture control lights. The Romex cable is run throughout the home by drilling holes through the wood structure as necessary. In some cases, each hole must then be filled to meet fire code separation requirements.[14] Typical installation results in wires that are hidden behind drywall and are difficult to locate later. Even if they are located and the drywall is removed, wiring can still be very difficult to remove or replace without destroying the structure. Moving an outlet can require many of the same tasks as moving a wall: removing drywall, possibly removing structure, replacing drywall, spackling, priming, and re-painting. On the other hand, moving a wall requires the relocation of any utilities that were run through that wall, which can be a significant task. The coupled nature of the structure, finish, and utilities can be problematic.

2.3.3 Data Distribution
Data cabling is installed in a similar manner to electrical cabling. Coaxial and unshielded twisted pair cable is typically used to carry data. Unlike the electrical system, data is usually run to only a few locations. This leads to a high probability that additional wiring and terminations may be required in the future. Unfortunately, adding new data outlets can be just as difficult as adding new electrical outlets. One potential benefit for disentanglement in this area is the advent of wireless data transmission, which decouples data transmission from the structure and finish by making wiring unnecessary. Wireless transmission is especially suited to adding data distribution to an existing home because of the difficulty of running new wires. However, even wireless systems still require an access point to the data services (modem, input cable, etc.) that must be located and wired.

2.3.4 Water Distribution and Sewerage
Plumbing may consist of copper, cross-linked polyethylene (PEX), chlorinated polyvinylchloride (CPVC), or polyvinyl chloride (PVC) piping (see Figure 10). Copper, CPVC, and PVC are rigid and require fittings to be routed around corners. Unlike copper components, which are generally

---

[14] Al Marzullo, TKG East Engineering, personal interview, January 2004.

soldered to each other, CPVC and PVC are glued together.[15] PEX piping is more flexible than copper or PVC and can be connected with a variety of mechanical deformation fasteners.[16] As in the case of electrical and data wiring, plumbing is generally run though holes drilled in the wood structure as necessary. Unfortunately, pipes are generally much larger than wires and therefore require larger holes that can weaken the structure. In the case of inflexible copper or PVC piping, it is virtually impossible to remove or relocate a system once it is in place. The connections are difficult to detach, and the rigid pipe is often embedded in the structure. Flexible piping, such as PEX, is easier to remove or relocate, but drilling holes can still cause structural damage. Fire suppression systems use similar plumbing technology, but currently are only common in attached construction. They represent an example of a utility system that could see expand use in the future.

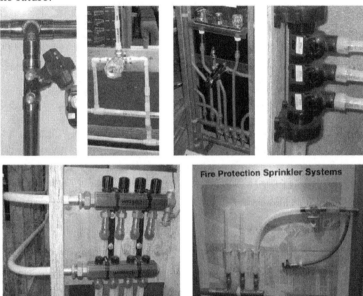

Clockwise from top left: traditional soldered copper pipe, glued CPVC, PEX and copper, PEX with plastic fittings, PEX with metal fittings, and PEX used for sprinkler systems. Photos from International Builders Show.
Figure 10: Plumbing Technologies

2.3.5 HVAC Distribution

HVAC systems present challenges to disentanglement, because they are generally very inflexible, and require a large amount of space (see Figure 11). Most homes built in the United States today use a forced air system to provide both heating and cooling.[17] The supply air is usually distributed though rigid metal ducting, although flexible metal ducts are used in some situations.[18] Generally, horizontal distribution of ductwork is done in the basement or attic and vertical distribution is done in closets or specially constructed areas. In some instances, soffits or other special structures must be built for distribution. This can become a problem in three-story homes, when the basement is finished, or when a forced air system is installed in an existing

---

[15] FlowGuardGold product literature.
[16] Survey of International Building Conference manufacturers.
[17] A Look at Residential Energy Consumption in 1997, DOE Report, 1997.
[18] Nelson Olivera, Nelson Group Construction, personal interview, December 2003.

home.[19] Before central AC, the traditional method of heating the house from a central location was with water (hydronic system). The water in today's designs is run through copper or plastic pipes, terminating at either baseboard or in-floor radiant heaters. In such cases, small room or mini-split AC units installed in walls or windows, requiring no ducting system, can provide air conditioning. Unfortunately, room units are often louder and less aesthetically pleasing than centralized systems.

From left to right: PEX radiant heating embedded in sub floor, PEX radiant heating embedded in concrete, traditional ductwork for forced air heating, and flexible gas pipe and a fitting. Photos from International Builders Show.
Figure 11: Heating and Gas Technologies

2.3.6 Gas Distribution

Gas is run though homes using rigid black iron pipe, copper tubing, or flexible stainless steel (CSST) pipe. As in the case with plumbing, holes are drilled though the structure to route the gas piping, as necessary. Gas distribution presents all of the same challenges as water piping. It is difficult to remove or relocate, can compromise structure, and takes a significant amount of space.

In summary, there are several reasons to conclude that the current utility technologies do not lend themselves to disentangled solutions or easy remodeling. However, the methods of installation and organization of the construction process itself could be even more important to disentanglement than the distribution technologies used. This further complication is discussed in the following sections.

2.4 Building Systems in Use Today

While most of the homes constructed today continue to be stick built, a variety of other building systems are now available. Certain methods have been successful in specific markets, because each method offers unique advantages and disadvantages. The basic characteristics of each building method and how they may affect disentangling will be discussed in this section. While many builders mix these methods or use different methods for different projects, we will treat each method individually here for the sake of simplicity. How builders and contractors use these methods and the business models that surround these building systems will be discussed in Section 3.2. The opportunity for disentanglement and the need for disentanglement of each business model will be covered in some detail. Suggestions for where disentangling efforts might be most beneficial and effective will be presented in Section 4.

---

[19] Al Marzullo, TKG East Engineering, personal interview, January 2004.

2.4.1 Stick-Built Homes

Figure 12: Stick-Building Construction

Stick-built homes employ individual members as structure elements, put together in much the same way they have been for decades. This system delivers acceptable quality at relatively low cost. Framing is constructed on-site by cutting and assembling lumber and is generally then erected by hand. This method is often mixed with panelized construction (Section 2.4.2) by building trusses and framing off-site. Utilities are added after the structure is complete by drilling through the framing and fitting systems into wall and floor cavities. The framing is overbuilt, which usually allows for this type of intrusion without catastrophic results. Generally, only the end points of utility runs are carefully planned. This can result in problematic situations, such as pinch points and conflicts, which usually are overcome through a repetitive process and/or rework. Insulation and finish are fit over and around utilities, completely sealing them into the building. These homes are built using intensive craft-based labor in a repetitive process that allows issues caused by entangled utilities to be dealt with in a prototype and eliminated. In the case of custom homes, which lack the repetition to allow for optimization, costs can quickly rise, in part because of the entangled utility problem.

2.4.2 Panelized Construction

Figure 13: Panelized Building during Construction

Panelized construction is another home building method, which uses factory built panels that are assembled on site. Roof trusses, wall frames, and SIPs fall into this group. Panels can range from a simple open wooden frame; similar to what would be built on-site, to a fully closed wall complete with windows, doors, and interior and exterior finishes. Because panelized

19

construction still relies heavily on traditional site-built methods, the gain in efficiency falls far short of a complete building system designed specifically for this type of factory-based of construction. The most complex and problematic field operations – such as installation of windows, doors, exterior and interior finishes, drywall, and all mechanical, electrical, communication, and plumbing systems – are typically still performed on-site in the conventional manner. The building produced is often generic, difficult to repair and remodel, and relatively low tech, comparable to traditional stick-built tract homes.

Most builders who use open panelized (unfinished) systems handle utilities in the same manner as they would for a traditional stick-built home. However, closed panelized construction methods place constraints on utility placement, which may actually lead to disentangling. In SIPs, the solid core allows no space for utilities that have not been planned. As a result, there is additional emphasis on designing with utilities in mind, which pushes disentanglement concerns forward. One solution to this problem is the addition of simple raceways dedicated to utility distribution. Raceways impose organization and may allow easy access for repair or limited modification. By using raceways and dedicated utility cores, builders provide a dedicated decoupled space. But this space is often generic and ill suited to the needs of every situation, thus still requiring material to be removed to allow for utility installation. Furthermore, utilities are almost always still hidden behind drywall and other non-removable finishes, making access impossible and obscuring the run locations. Making utility changes in panelized construction is often more difficult than in stick built, because, in addition to lack of access and location information, creating new space for utilities is more challenging.

2.4.3 Modular Homes

Figure 14: Modular Housing under Construction

Modular construction moves most field operations to the controlled environment of a factory, eliminating weather concerns, and allowing use of better tools and more efficient quality control. This industry represents 7% of the total U.S. housing market.[20] Modular homes are built in large three-dimensional sections, which are typically 95% complete when they leave the factory.[21] The modules are then transported to the site and placed, by crane, onto a permanent foundation where

---

[20] Traynor, T., "Total Housing Even in 2001 at 2.219 million," Automated Builder, 39(1), January 2002.
[21] Carson, D. (ed), 1991, Automated Builder: Dictionary/Encyclopedia of Industrialized Housing, Automated Builder Magazine, Publications Division, CMN Associates, Inc., Carpinteria, CA.

final construction is completed. These homes are generally indistinguishable in appearance from conventionally built homes. Unfortunately, part of being indistinguishable from conventional homes is not allowing access to utilities for change over time or for integrating new technologies. However, the modular construction process can be significantly more efficient than developer construction. It is possible to avoid many of the problems of entangled utilities in this construction system. Because the houses must be fully designed before construction, the utility runs and locations are typically better planned. This system generally also has some attractive business characteristics for disentangling, which will be discussed further in Section 3.2.

2.4.4 Manufactured Housing

Figure 15: Manufactured Housing Module during Transport

Manufactured housing is similar to modular housing, except that manufactured houses are completely finished at the factory and follow the national HUD-code rather than regional building codes. As such, manufactured housing has many of the same benefits that exist for modular housing. HUD-code manufactured homes are typically smaller and less expensive than other modular homes, and are technically moveable, although once placed on a site they can be indistinguishable.[22] One advantage of HUD-code manufactured homes when disentangling utilities is that they have uniform code requirements. Unlike the model national code, the HUD-code is binding and does not require local adoption or enforcement. This can allow disentangling technologies to be more easily implemented, because once a product or method is adopted into the HUD-code, it is accepted. The International Code Council (ICC) Evaluation Service can approve products or methods to be included in the national model code, but state and local code officials may still refuse to accept the product or method at their own discretion. A performance-based code would avoid the need for national approval of specific products or methods but is difficult to administer, and many communities are hesitant to accept the responsibility of doing so. Furthermore, a prescriptive code allows residential builders a simpler prediction of what code officials will accept and what they won't. However, if the performance-based code could be designed to be easily enforceable by a local inspector and easily understood by builders, it could allow for innovation with less bureaucracy.

---

[22] Factory and Site-Built Housing: A Comparison for the 21st Century, NAHB, 1998.

3   Technical Analysis of Entanglement in Housing

This section builds upon the background information covered in Section 2 with more detailed analysis of the most important issues and relationships. This analysis is divided into three areas, physical relationships, business models and perspectives, and the marketplace and industry situation. This provides a more extensive problem statement to frame the future strategies that will be outlined in Section 4.

3.1   Physical Situation and Barriers: Mapping Functional Integration

Three ways to map utilities to functions in a home were investigated. The first is by delivery-- how utilities are brought to the user, the second by construction – how the home is built and how utilities are installed, and the third by interaction – how people interface with utility systems.[23] These mappings help to analyze and evaluate disentanglement strategies.

3.1.1   Delivery Model[24]

In Figure 16, the delivery model starts with "Public Utilities" and ends with "Returns/Exits" (such as waste water and exhaust gases). It should be noted that individual companies usually supply public utilities, such as electricity, water, and gas, whereas telecommunication services can involve multiple companies (Internet, TV, phone and security). In the diagram, "Unit Operations" refer to units such as filters for water treatment, furnaces for heating, and air conditioners for cooling. "Appliances" include refrigerators, stoves, dishwashers, etc. This model can be used to categorize the issues related to a given utility and focus on one area, while maintaining a global view of how changes in that area might affect the other parts of the delivery system. This report focuses primarily on in-home distribution, but it is important to be aware of the relationship of in-home distribution to the rest of the system.

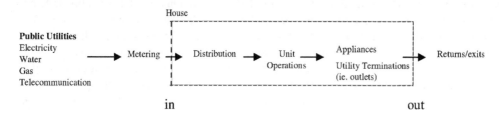

Figure 16: Utility Delivery Process

Table 2 describes the relationship among public utilities, utilities in the home, usable end points, and home spaces. Column 1 identifies public utilities coming into a home and column 2 shows how these utilities are converted, transformed, or redistributed into services. Columns 3 and 4 show types of termination points (outlets or appliances) and the areas in the home where those terminations might be located.

---

[23] The data model used in this section is shown in the appendix.

[24] The organization of the table and the categories shown are part of a process for evaluating solutions.

1. Public Utilities	2. Utilities in the Home	3. End Points	4. Areas
Electricity	Electricity (distribution panel; GFI, lightning, surge, overload)	Outlets, lights, appliances, furnace	All areas
Telecommunication	Data	Phone jacks, set-tops, data ports	Main living areas
Water	Water, treated (filtered, sterilized, deionized)	Faucets, refrigerator, washer, dishwasher	Kitchen, bath, laundry
Water/gas	Hot water	Faucets, washer, dishwasher	Kitchen, bath, laundry
Sewer	Wastewater (cooking, washing, vents, drains)	Sinks, toilets, dishwasher, washer	Kitchen, bath, laundry
Data/control	Fire detection (smoke, CO, heat)	Sensors/detectors	Each floor
Water	Fire protection (sprinkler)	Sprinkler heads	All areas
Data/control	Security (motion, glass, egress)	Sensors/detectors	Access and egress points
Electricity, gas	Heating, cooling	Registers	All areas
Electricity	Ventilation, exhaust air		Kitchen, baths, drier
Fuel (gas, oil, gasoline)	Emergency power	Distribution panel	Outside
	Rain water shedding	Gutters, leaders	Outside, inside
Electricity	Central vacuum	Vacuum outlet/exhaust	

Table 2: Public Utilities to Functional Areas in a Home

3.1.2 Construction Model

A construction model of home utilities identifies the trades involved and thus the way infrastructure systems are built and installed.

Infrastructure System	Trades
Foundation & structure	Cement, finisher, framer, excavator, landscaper
Weatherproofing (enclosure)	Framer, roofer, painter
Water/wastewater	Plumber
Gray water	Plumber, excavator
Communication/data	Telecom installer, electrician
HVAC	Electrician, sheet metal bender, mechanical technician
Electricity & lighting	Electrician
Security & safety	Electrician, telecom installer, specialist -security installer
Fire protection	Plumber, specialist -fire protection installer

Table 3: Construction Systems and Trades

Understanding the construction process (see Section 2) and how systems are installed can lead to the development of potential solutions to the entanglement problem.

The trades can physically interfere with one another by installing systems in shared space. The workers may not be able to share the space effectively and may be forced to schedule their work at different times. The installed utilities themselves can also conflict. However, more significant than the physical situation is the problem of how the stakeholders interact and the effect of combining their various perspectives. This will be discussed further in Section 3.2.

3.1.3 Interaction Model

The following table relates functional end-use systems to appliances and the supporting infrastructure systems. Changes to infrastructure will affect what functional end-use systems are possible or feasible. Conversely, changes to functional systems or the addition of potential new systems, such as those mentioned in Section 1.1 (distributed power generation, preventative health care, learning, etc.), will require new infrastructure systems. Appliances are the link between infrastructure and end use.

Functional end-use systems	Appliances	Infrastructure system
Food and nutrition	Stove, refrigerator, microwave, dishwasher, garbage disposal	Water/wastewater, electrical, HVAC
Clean clothes	Washer, dryer	Water/wastewater, electrical, gray water
Personal hygiene	Electric toothbrush, hairdryer, electric razor	Water/wastewater
Entertainment/ social	Computer, stereo, TV, audio system, phone, answering machine	Electrical, communication
Environmental control	Air/allergen filters, thermostat	HVAC
Lighting	Portable and built-in fixtures	Electrical
Safety	Alarms, displays	Security, safety, fire protection

Table 4: Functional Systems, Appliances, and Infrastructure Systems

Understanding how appliances link end uses to infrastructure can help predict the future demands that will be placed on the infrastructure. Watching for new appliance developments will give a short-term prediction of future infrastructure needs, and watching up-and-coming end uses will give a longer-term prediction. Additional infrastructure requirements will further complicate the aggregate system and make disentanglement even more important.

3.2 Stakeholders: Utility Disentanglement Viewed from Multiple Perspectives

The intent of this section is to develop a framework for how firms in the housing industry are organized, which segments of the market they address, their strategies for production, and their incentives/disincentives for deploying non-standard, disentangled utility solutions. This analysis overlaps, but does not match exactly the building-method discussion in Section 2.4, because the most useful division of firms and stakeholders when discussing disentanglement is not strictly by building technology or system. For example, the factory-based builder of custom homes could use a panelized, modular, or a manufactured housing method and still have similar disentanglement opportunities.

The process of integrating wire, pipes, and ducts into conventional, speculative, stick-built housing is well understood and generally standardized across the United States. In fact, many suburban merchant builders might question whether there is a problem with utility entanglement at all. However, there are emerging factory-based strategies for housing production in the United States that rely on further utility disentanglement for success. Issues related to utility disentanglement, therefore, must be seen from the many perspectives of those affected and by how utilities are designed and installed – during both construction and use after occupancy. The following overview of stakeholder perspectives will be used to establish focus and identify criteria for possible disentanglement strategies.

There are thousands of homebuilders in the United States, ranging from small custom builders that produce several houses per year to large merchant builders/developers that create tens of thousands per year. Businesses are structured in a variety of ways that depend on the target market, business objectives, building technology, labor sources, organizational depth, and management practices. Proposed technical solutions for improving how utilities are designed and installed in homes will likely be incomplete if the complexity of the U.S. home building industry is not taken into account. Although there are many variations and hybrids, using a variety of building systems, the following describes the four basic strategic approaches to home building.

3.2.1   The Site-Based Builder of Speculative Generic Homes (Merchant Builders)

Overview:
While generic speculative housing developments are rare in Northern Europe and Japan, most of the new housing built in the United States falls into this category. Major merchant homebuilders include Centex, Pulte, and Lenner. Generally, these companies operate regionally or nationally, moving from site to site as land is acquired. They operate as landowners and housing developers, building standardized commodity homes in all price ranges. The typical process involves acquiring a relatively large parcel of land, securing local permits for the development, commissioning a market study to identify the "bull's-eye" at the center of the market, using or adapting several standard house models that best fit the market, producing prototypes to work out details and coordinate with subcontractors, mass producing standard house models on site, and marketing and selling the product. Customer involvement tends to be limited to a relatively few choices, such as finishes, fixtures, and appliances.

Merchant builders typically have little in-house production capability, and the process relies on local subcontractors using the traditional, labor-intensive techniques of stick-built housing. Panelization occurs in some instances, but the vast majority of the work is performed on-site. The builders operate in a wide range of localities and, therefore, can't always use the same subcontractors with whom they have worked previously. Most, if not all, of the actual construction work is performed by independent subcontractors. The subcontractors competitively bid on work packages that have been defined by drawings and specifications prepared by others. This process encourages local subcontractors to develop ingenious cost-saving strategies tailored to their particular labor force, available technology, and scale of operation. Since each mechanical, electrical, and plumbing (MEP) trade conducts its work in the field independently, layer-by-layer, after the frame is completed, the resulting wires, ducts, and pipes tend to be entangled within the structure.

Since this system relies on local independent subcontractors, there is a clear incentive for the developer to specify widely familiar, standard construction materials and practices. Inevitably, the introduction of any new and unfamiliar materials or techniques will require additional training and "learning-curve" delays. Because the subcontractors bid on a completed design, they have little opportunity or incentive to introduce significant innovations into the design or the process. Since each subcontractor is also contractually obligated to guarantee the quality and performance of the work, there is a tendency to resist new ideas that may result in unanticipated consequences. Since profit margins tend to be low, subcontractors can be highly innovative to improve the efficiency of their particular operations (such as prefabricating water supply piping assemblies), but they rarely coordinate innovation with other independent subcontractors. As a result, there is little incentive to develop the home, and the utilities in particular, as an integrated system.

At each development site, specialized crews move from house to house in a highly efficient, mass production process. Typically, when a new model is introduced, a prototype house is built where a representative of each utility subcontractor can work with the development team to resolve conflicts and establish highly efficient work patterns. The resulting wires, ducts, and pipes may be fully "entangled," in that holes are drilled through walls and floor structures and utilities are intertwined with each other. This is done in a highly coordinated fashion intended to expedite low-cost installation with a minimum of coordination overhead.

While the developers are in a position to direct choices in the building process, it is difficult for them to realize returns from process or technology improvements that could actually increase the bottom line of individual subcontractors. Even if a disentangling innovation requested by the developer has the potential to lower cost for a subcontractor, the subcontractor may still raise their price due to uncertainty. This disconnect impedes disentanglement because the key player, the developer in this case, is not able to capture its value.[25]

Homebuyers, of course, are highly sensitive to purchase price. Speculative builders, therefore, strive to build the lowest-cost home possible with sufficient quality to achieve the desired sale price. Homebuyers are also typically more concerned about initial sale price than life-cycle costs. As a result, there is a disincentive to develop new materials, systems, and processes that might improve life-cycle costs (ease of renovation, repair, and upgrade during the occupancy of the house), but increase the sale price. Builders may innovate, but their innovations tend to be limited to those that decrease their building costs. The builders interviewed largely believe they have optimized their utility installation methods through repetition. For them, installing utilities in a planned, organized, and accessible way was viewed as unnecessary and costly.[26] The key notion of separating utilities from the structure was believed to be difficult to achieve because of their building system and past experience.

Also, since builders rarely participate in the service, upgrade, and retrofit of the homes they build, they place the highest value on initial quality and cost. There is almost no emphasis on ownership costs and making the home easy to service, upgrade, and retrofit. The post-occupancy

[25] Jim Petersen, Pulte Home Sciences, personal interview, January 2004.

[26] Randy Luther, Centex Homes, personal interview, February 2004 .

benefits of disentangled utilities are, therefore, not a focus in the marketing and sales of speculative home developments.

Disentanglement Potential:
Since housing developers are not incentivized to encourage disentanglement innovation among the hundreds of plumbers, electricians, HVAC contractors, and carpenters on whom they rely when entering a new market, process-changing disentangling innovations will likely come slowly and incrementally to this industry. The cost and overhead for training and coordination, and likely increases in bid prices for new practices – even if demonstratively more efficient – creates powerful disincentives for disentanglement innovation. Since customers (homebuyers) have little direct input into the design and production of these commodity homes, the market forces driving innovation for the customer are limited. Large merchant builders, therefore, will likely be slower to adopt innovative disentangling practices than might be expected for similar innovations in other consumer industries, such as automotive or appliances. Smaller, more factory-based housing production firms (see Section 3.2.4) and custom-home builders will likely be the first to attempt and successfully implement innovative disentangling practices in housing.

On a more positive note, looking to the future and following trends in other industries, large merchant home builders could form "value networks" with trusted outsourcing partners who will pre-negotiate performance-based solutions in lieu of bidding. Such a process would place a premium on collaboration, innovation, and coordination, and encourage a movement away from smaller, independent subcontractors towards consolidation and vertical integration. This would also expedite the adoption of new systems and processes that increase efficiency, quality, performance, and serviceability.

3.2.2   The Site-Based Builder of Custom Homes

Overview:
This small but growing segment of residential housing, together with the factory builder of generic homes and the factory-based builder of custom homes described in the next two sections, offer perhaps the best potential for initially realizing benefit from disentangling. Once the advantages are demonstrated and realized here, the opportunity may arise to see these benefits flow to the higher volume segment of the housing industry. Although more independent and flexible than the merchant developers, the builders of higher-end custom homes using conventional site-based construction processes experience many of the same constraints as the large speculative builders. They rely on local subcontractors and have many of the same disincentives for disentanglement innovation. However, there are three major points of distinction: custom builders have a more intimate relationship with the homebuyer, they do not build prototypes, since they produce "one-off" houses, and they generally operate exclusively in a local area with longer-term relationships with subcontractors.

Disentanglement Potential:
Since custom builders work with individual clients to develop a design that reflects their needs, values, and dreams, there are often customer-based pressures to innovate. The custom builder and the client can engage in a discussion of initial cost and life cycle cost tradeoffs, and issues, such as maintenance, durability, ease of upgrade, etc. This can encourage the incorporation of utility disentanglement. Since the custom builder does not benefit from first building a

prototype, a higher value is placed on solutions that make the building processes more predictable and less dependent on keeping highly varied and entangled systems carefully coordinated. Finally, since custom builders tend to have long-term relationships with local subcontractors, there is more opportunity to coordinate multi-disciplinary innovation. Site-based custom builders may therefore introduce novel materials and processes more readily than the larger, speculative developers.

3.2.3   The Factory-Based Builder of Custom Homes

Overview:
Although rare in the United States, fully customized housing built from pre-finished wall, floor, and roof components is increasingly common in Europe and Japan. Companies that have successfully deployed this approach include Grifnerhaus (Austria), Sekesui Homes (Japan), Toyota Homes (Japan), and Bensonwood Homes (USA). A growing number of companies also offer semi-customized factory-built kit homes, which may or may not use pre-finished components. These companies generally use a variation of the open building system (Section 2.2.2), and panelization (Section 2.4.2).

This approach is based on developing highly efficient processes that move otherwise labor-intensive field operations into the controlled environment of the factory where repetition, predictability, quality control, and economies of scale can more readily be realized. In the more advanced operations, emphasis is placed on pre-finished wall, floor, and roof elements. The production facilities generally serve a local or regional area to minimize shipping costs. These companies usually have in-house installation crews trained in non-standard operations or a network of specialist sub-contractors familiar with the building system. Since each home is unique, there is no opportunity to develop a whole-house prototype to coordinate the various trades. Instead, companies carefully develop design protocols, prototypical connections, and production assemblies that can be combined in varied, but predictable, ways.

Disentanglement Potential:
Companies producing pre-finished components for prefabricated custom homes have the greatest incentive to develop and apply new approaches to disentangling home utilities. The most innovative companies have developed wall, floor, and roof components with standard chases and raceways for wire, plumbing, and ductwork. They have sought innovative MEP components, such as snap-fit plumbing connectors; plug-in electrical connections, that do not require junction boxes or wire nuts; hydronic heating systems that can be pre-installed in enclosure components; and integrated wall, floor, and ceiling plenums for supply and return air that do not require field-installed ductwork. Since these custom-home producers typically work intimately with individual home buyers during the design process, there is an opportunity to introduce end-users to the potential advantages of new systems that can reduce life-cycle costs – and save costs and minimize disruptions related to upgrading equipment, altering the home later on, and maintaining and repairing systems. Even more significant, the trades often work together in parallel under one management system, which allows for better coordination. In addition, there are sometimes formalized methods for capturing innovation. When a process improvement is made, the factory-based building company is more likely to realize the profits than is the developer in the tract-home scenario. All the trades' people working on the home are typically employees of the company. This allows for a team approach that emphasizes total process efficiency and

profitability, instead of the efficiency and profitability of small pieces of the process.[27] Whole-house solutions, which may negatively impact the cost of one part of the structure but improve the overall cost, can therefore be considered.

3.2.4 The Factory-Based Builder of Generic Homes

Overview:
The idea of mass-producing homes using a factory-based approach similar to automobile or appliance manufacturing has been around since the turn of the century. Although never fully achieved in practice, there have been some successful efforts at moving home production into a factory and producing a repeatable product. Today, workable strategies for factory-based generic home production use three different systems: modular homes (Section 2.4.3), manufactured homes (section 2.4.4), and new versions of mostly entry-level "kit homes," which may include panels (section 2.4.2) or employ some other building system. Modular homes are often built in fully finished volumetric modules at a factory – complete with lighting, electric, HVAC systems, and plumbing. Modules, limited by the size constraints of highway transportation, are shipped to the home site on truck beds and then joined in the field. Manufactured homes are built in a factory on a non-removable steel chassis, conform to federal (HUD) – rather than local – building codes, and are transported to the home site on their own wheels. A variety of "kit homes," including the popular timber log house, are available. Kit homes often include just the shell wall panels, floor decks, roof and floor trusses, roof sheathing, and exterior doors and windows with the finishes and utilities conventionally installed in the field. Others offer "full packages," including MEP systems and finishes.

Disentanglement Potential:
Unlike site-built homes, factory-built housing can introduce disentanglement innovations in the controlled environment of the factory, with an in-house labor force that can be more efficiently trained to accommodate new materials, systems, and processes. In essence, this in-house labor is both builder and subcontractor, which allows for better control and more efficient management, especially during a period of change or innovation. Factory-built generic-housing manufacturers can, in principle, more easily standardize processes than factory-built custom homebuilders because the range of product offerings is more limited. Some of the more innovative processes can be found in the production of entry-level manufactured homes. However, because they target more sophisticated customers, these homes are more expensive and have higher margins. Our interviews showed that custom factory-built homes are well ahead in the adoption of innovative disentangled utility solutions.

3.2.5 The Component Manufacturer's Perspective

Overview:
While component manufacturers in other industries assume greater and greater responsibility for incorporating new materials, technologies, and design ideas into the products they provide to the integrators and assemblers, the opposite is true in the housing industry. "Builders continue to buy

---

[27] Ray Cudwadie, Deluxe Homes, personal interview, January 2004.

'cheaper' products, installed with less skilled labor."[28] "The component manufacturer, forced to lower price points, cuts material costs, strips away features, puts less engineering and R&D into products, reduces services. The building industry is hamstrung by conventional thinking that defines the building process as random collections of isolated products. Not as an integrated system." This is unfortunate since component manufacturers are often diversified companies with the resources and expertise to engage in research that will result in innovation. They also have much to gain from positively affecting building codes to accommodate and promote innovative new utility technologies.

Disentanglement Potential:
There is no shortage of new design ideas, innovative systems, new materials, and new processes that could be applied to housing. These can be found in proven innovations from other industries, from emerging innovations in building science from overseas, and in countless products ideas developed in the United States that have not found their way to market. To realize this potential, the incentives for innovation must be clearly identified and promoted. In addition, innovative manufacturers should move towards integrated solutions that solve multiple problems simultaneously.

3.2.6   The Alteration Contractor's Perspective

Overview:
Billions of dollars are spent each year on home rehab, alteration, and upgrade. Most alteration work is performed by small "handyman" contractors or by the homeowners themselves (reflected in the success of Home Depot and Lowes). Conventional home-construction methods and the entanglement of wires, pipes, and ducts into the structure of the home make the process of demolition, alteration, and system upgrade complicated, expensive, time consuming, and disruptive.

Disentanglement Potential:
Many homebuilders are dissatisfied with their inability to effectively participate in the alteration of homes after occupancy. Simple strategies, such as keeping pipes and wires out of walls that may be demolished in the future (between the master and child's bedroom, for example), would significantly reduce the cost and complexity of alteration. More advanced products that allow for rapid reconfiguration, such as snap-fit plumbing or rapid-connect electrical devices, could create new alteration-related business opportunities for larger homebuilders. In addition, these advances could also create more profitable business opportunities for services related to maintenance and system repair/upgrade.

3.2.7   The Subcontractors Perspective

Overview:
Typically, tradesmen functioning as independent contractors install MEP utilities. These subcontractors bid competitively on work defined by others through drawings and specifications. If these subcontractors innovate (and this is rare), they limit their innovation to materials and

---

[28] The Partnership for Advanced Technology in Housing (PATH), in a report prepared by NAHB Research Center, March 2001

processes that affect only the work for which they are under contract. Any possible improvements are highly constrained by the drawings and specifications that define their scope of work – resulting mainly in small, incremental improvements to standard processes.

Disentanglement Potential:
There is an emerging trend in the construction industry towards consolidation and the creation of larger, more capable companies that can deploy more sophisticated processes, quality control, and new technologies. Our discussions with builders indicate that the future will inevitably involve a movement from subcontracts to partnerships, with each party providing integrated solutions within "value networks." This would greatly encourage collaboration, innovation, coordination, and vertical integration with broad benefits accruing to both the industry and the homeowner.

3.2.8 Considerations in the Business Case for Disentanglement

The applicability of disentanglement solutions, and the extent to which utility entanglement is considered a problem in the first place, depends on a complex mix of characteristics of the builder in question, including:
- Degree of customization ("build-to-suit" vs. "build-on-spec")
- Degree of prefabrication (site built vs. factory built)
- Market served: price point (entry vs. mid-range vs. luxury)
- Market served: generational (seniors vs. baby boomers vs. young families)
- Percentage of in-house labor (local subcontractors vs. specially trained employees)
- Territory of operation (local vs. regional vs. national)
- Single family vs. multifamily

These characteristics can lead to higher or lower concern for the attributes that disentangling utilities can provide:

- Reduced material cost
- Reduced field labor
- Greater ease of factory manufacturing
- Ease of repair
- Ease of upgrade
- Ease of removal
- Longer building life-spans
- Lower life-cycle cost

The higher the value placed on these attributes, the greater the likelihood that that particular stakeholder will be open to change (See Table 5). The table can also help map a particular strategy for each stakeholder.

	End User - Homeowner	MEP Sub-contractor	Maintenance Technician	Alteration Contractor	Builder: Site Based / Generic	Builder: Site Based / Custom	Builder: Factory-Based/ Generic	Builder: Factory-Based / Custom
Reduced Material Cost	-	***	-	-	***	***	*	*
Reduced Field Labor	-	***	-	-	***	***	***	***
Factory Compatible	-	*	-	-	-	-	***	***
Ease of Repair	***	-	***	-	-	**	-	**
Ease of Upgrade	***	-	***	-	-	**	-	**
Ease of Removal	***	-	***	***	-	-	-	**
Life Span of System	***	-	***	-	*	**	*	**
Low Life Cycle Costs	***	-	-	-	*	**	*	**
Total Value of Improved Utilities	15	7	12	3	8	14	9	17

Table 5: Approximate Value of Utility Attribute for Stakeholders
*** = High value placed; ** = Medium value placed; * = Low value placed; - = Not a significant concern

3.3 Marketplace and Industry Situation and Barriers to Innovation

In this continuing analysis and problem statement based on the history and situation presented in Section 2, barriers to disentanglement will be examined. Barriers to innovation exist at three levels: marketplace, industry, and the firm.

3.3.1 General Marketplace Barriers

Five barriers common to all industries are:

- Too large a change can produce a myriad of unintended consequences and side effects that often block implementation.

- If the people affected by the change do not receive enough support to become proficient in the use of the innovation, it will be rejected or not used to its full potential.

- If the innovators fail to address the unique physical, technological and cognitive limits of the workplace and work force—the innovation will not fit and will be rejected.

- Important contextual factors that support an innovation in one area may be missing from another area resulting in failure of the innovation.

- Integration of the new with the old is often neglected and, as a result, the innovation fails.

3.3.2 Industry Specific Barriers

The housing industry is loosely coupled, highly interdependent, and very stable with a large infrastructure of support. In this type of industry, the size, scale, and scope of change is important, and comprehensive and effective communication is vital. Specific barriers include the following:

3.3.2.1 Size of Possible Variation is Small

The larger the change, the more related areas would be affected. If these additional unanticipated or anticipated effects are outside localized areas of control, the change is likely to fail. Successful innovation can occur by limiting the extent of change. As an example, consider the automobile industry, which is similar to the housing industry in that both have large support infrastructures. For vehicles, this infrastructure includes highway service and maintenance organizations, gasoline stations, tires and battery services. A large change that remained within the boundaries of control in this industry is the development of the hybrid engine for the Toyota Prius and the Honda Insight and is described below:

> Both these cars employ a small gasoline engine and a small electric engine that work together to power the car. For years the automobile industry had been trying to develop an all-electric car. An all-electric car would require a battery of sufficient size; fast charging stations, locations for these charging stations, etc. But in the Prius or Insight, the electric engine is contained within the boundaries of the car's engine compartment and requires no manual charging—charging occurs during braking. The amount of time when the electric motor must be run by batteries is small and thus the system demands little charging and small batteries. The driver operates the car in the same way that he operates an all-gasoline car. In this case innovation occurred within a set of constraints requiring few changes by the customer and support-service organizations.

3.3.2.2 Lack of Adequate Information Exchange (Instructive Burden)

For a firm to be competitive in the building industry, communication must be effective and efficient. In successful firms, the order and sequence of activities is well known and repeated many times. Little explicit communication is required. But any change from the routine requires a significant amount of communication, which raises the risk of miscommunication and error and - even more importantly - takes time. To be successful, an innovation must not overly increase the complexity of the communication process.

3.3.2.3 The U.S. Housing Industry has been Slow to Learn from Related Industries

It is illuminating to compare cruise-ship building, passenger aircraft production, and automotive manufacturing to new housing development. Each involves the functional integration of many materials and systems to create environments for people. In these other industries, manufacturers operate from large central production facilities where they can introduce innovation from the "top down" in a controlled manner, or absorb and coordinate innovation developed by large and sophisticated Tier-1 suppliers from the "bottom up." Manufacturers in these industries are rapidly moving towards highly mechanized production of modular components and subcomponents. Cruise-ship production, for example, often assembles the hull in modular sections and inserts prefabricated cabins custom fit to the changing curvature of the form - with rapid-connect utilities preinstalled. In each of these industries, there is a trend to off-load innovation to Tier-1 suppliers, who are increasingly sophisticated in their application of new materials, digital technologies, supply-chain management, information technologies, and highly efficient automated manufacturing processes. With global competition, innovation introduced in Europe, for example, is quickly emulated in the United States, Japan, and Korea.

Japanese housing, and to a lesser extent that of Northern Europe, is rapidly moving towards automated factory-based manufacturing of increasingly customized homes designed and built for individual clients. These approaches to housing are beginning to parallel trends in the production of cars, planes, and cruise ships in that the process is highly mechanized and factory based. Modular components supplied by another company can contain innovations without disrupting the assembly process, and the assembling company can introduce general innovations in a controlled manner. See Appendix C for a more in-depth comparison of housing production systems and other industrial systems.

The U.S. building industry could learn much from the systems used in these related industries, but has so far failed to do so. It continues to use craft based, subcontracted, fragmented production systems that were long ago abandoned by other industries.

4   Future Strategies for Disentangling Utilities

Clearly, the potential exists to advance the way utilities are installed in homes. But how do we move from the current state to more efficient construction that utilizes disentangled utilities to reduce overall cost and increase functionality?

4.1   Review of Potential Opportunities and Emerging Needs

Before future strategies are discussed, it is useful to review the potential opportunities and emerging needs that have been identified so far. The functional mappings of delivery, building, and interaction, and the priorities of stakeholders developed in Section 3 are a framework for developing and evaluating the disentanglement strategies in this section.

A number of tools, components, and methods already exist that can be used in disentanglement. These include:
- Open joists for routing
- Vertical chases
- Drop ceiling for access
- Large centrally located open area acting as a plenum
- Well insulated enclosure—reduces heat and cooling loads
- Hydronic (hot water) heating using small diameter pipes
- Consolidated and stacked plumbing
- Integrated, combined venting
- Centralized plumbing manifolds
- Raceways built into exterior panels for electrical wiring
- Preplanned switch locations using conduit
- Coordination and planning tools for installation of public utilities
- Use of prototypes for training and analysis
- Subcontractor training and education
- On-site education and mentoring

But some problems persist or are difficult to solve:
- Communication and scheduling between trades working on different projects
- Rapid changes in telecommunication technologies make it difficult for builders to understand the best way of selecting and integrating services
- Oversight related to overall[29] quality (compliance to contract[30]) is difficult when there is a high workforce turnover rate

---

[29] Most builders pay close attention to quality and workmanship, but quality is a difficult attribute to define and measure and is often linked to measures of customer satisfaction.

[30] The many different firms contracted to build most homes each work under some kind of contract. Contracts typically specify cost, schedule, and work to be done, but not overall quality of the finished product.

New technologies and process improvements, such as the following, that may help alleviate entanglement issues already exist or are under development. But these need to be integrated into existing systems and processes.

- Addressable lighting
- Distributed HVAC
- New types of flexible piping
- Micro-CHP (combined heat and power systems)
- New types of media and communication technologies (see Appendix C)
- Ubiquitous computing technologies for location-based messaging
- Highly accurate positioning technologies (GPS)
- New collaborative applications with wireless connectivity for task-specific communication
- Display and projection technology
- Adoption of good manufacturing practices in the field (see in Appendix C)

Although entanglement may not be a high priority for current builders, new and unprecedented demands are continuously emerging in the market that will require homes to be quickly and easily adaptable and may change that thinking. There will be an increasing market for homes designed to accommodate new functions, for example the following, and *integrate* them into existing systems.

- Innovative health services—monitoring, controls, sensors, actuators, telecommunication
- Reliable power: emergency power needs for flexible and hard-wired equipment
- Better water quality and assurances (monitoring)
- Better air quality and assurances (monitoring)
- Enhanced personal safety and security
- Quality power for electronics
- Increased safety of the power system—grounding, ground fault, and lightning protection
- Improved environmental sustainability through conservation and load management, as well as the use of renewable energy

4.2   A Proposed Direction

In the past, those interested in a new home had two basic options: purchase a generic, standard design from a developer or engage an architect and builder to produce a tailored design option, with the risk of delays, overruns, errors, and omissions associated with a "one of a kind" project. A third option, becoming commonplace in Europe and Asia, has recently emerged in the United States: a predictable and cost-effective process of contracting for a custom home via one of several innovative companies that deploy advanced computational tools for design, fabrication, and supply-chain management. The potential for innovation is great and of interest to the HUD PATH Program, which is tasked with integrating new ideas and technology into housing to make it more affordable, functional, and reliable. This is not to imply that the benefits will be immediately realized in high volume, mass-produced, moderately priced housing, but that over time and with experience, these innovations will flow down.

Realization of this option's potential will require a coordinated effort in the following areas:

- Utility-Related Systems: Develop high performance, disentangled, low field-labor systems for heating, cooling, ventilation, plumbing, electrical distribution, and communication.

- Building Structure and Envelope: Develop industry standards for high performance, agile, rapid assembly, floor, wall, and roof components/connections that both minimize heating and cooling loads and provide predefined, accessible pathways for utilities.

- Software: Develop more effective software tools to streamline the process from design to product specification, manufacturing, scheduling, and assembly.

This new approach to improved housing is probably best described using a comprehensive scenario.

4.3 Scenario (Housing Industry in 2015)

The following four-part scenario provides an opportunity to further develop and understand a high-level, integrated view of a design and construction process that, for some portion of the housing industry, is possible to achieve in the next ten years. The reader is asked to accept the hypotheses as given and to consider the resulting outcomes. This scenario will be followed by a discussion of the pivotal role of utility disentanglement in transitioning to this future housing model.

4.3.1 Scenario: Developers and Integrators-Part I

Large residential land developers now specialize in the process of acquisition, financing, and navigation through increasingly complex public approval processes. These developers typically form business relationships with competing "builder-integrators," who manage the process of delivering individually tailored homes to the buyers of each lot. They are appropriately referred to as integrators, not builders, because they do not perform the same function as a traditional builder. They largely integrate high-value products manufactured by others and guide the assembly process to provide the desired solution for the homebuyer; they do little or no "building."

Competing head-to-head in a manner comparable to automobile and consumer electronics manufacturers, these integrators have evolved a highly efficient process of offering a wide range of styles, features, quality, and performance. The most successful excel in particular market niches. Mirroring the trend towards "Tier-1" suppliers in other industries, home building has evolved from field-labor processes organized by trade (subcontractors), to integrated "solutions" provided by outsourcing partners. Each integrator has relationships with a unique set of companies that provide the systems, products, and services that come together to make up their "branded" products. An explosion of creative energy in housing design, construction, and related services has been made possible by industry-wide agreement on standards for how components connect.

4.3.2 Scenario: Design, Configuration, and Industry Standards-Part II

Housing integrators have a variety of processes for helping customers arrive at a design. Some use a web "home configurator" with a constrained set of options – similar to what Dell developed for the mass customization of personal computers (PC). Other integrators specialize in one-on-one interaction with a specialist architect or para-architect to lead customers through the complex decision making process related to space planning, finishes, appliances, lighting, and future options. Most integrators offer thousands of possible combinations of elements, each with pricing, delivery schedule, etc., calculated in real time. As the buyer explores options, he or she is presented with tailored information – often directly from manufacturer's – to help in making informed decisions about cost, performance, aesthetics, life-cycle cost, and durability.

Regardless of the design and configuration strategy, all integrators capture the final design using computational tools that (manually or automatically) insert and manipulate industry-provided descriptions of each component – from bathroom fixtures to kitchen cabinets to HVAC equipment. These product descriptions include insertion points, three-dimensional sizes, and interface requirements to other subsystems. Although there are a wide variety of proprietary systems, the components all connect according to industry established standards. Power, data, water, gas, and floor/wall connections are largely interoperable among manufacturers – much as all USB devices for PCs share a standard interface. Companies that formerly produced commodity wood fiber building materials, now produce high-value building components, including integrated exterior wall, floor, roof, and interior infill systems. Companies that formerly produced pipe and wire, or proprietary fixtures or systems, now produce interoperable components for electrical, plumbing, HVAC systems - comparable to interchangeable devices in the PC industry.

4.3.3 Scenario: Fabrication and Utility Integration-Part III

When a house design is complete and the buyer transaction executed, data fully describing each of the components and systems is transmitted to the integrator's assembly factory. Each integrator takes advantage of supply-chain management tools similar to those developed in the automotive industry to receive just-in-time deliveries of required components from manufacturers and distributors. Although the systems of the house are carefully integrated, they also are carefully disentangled so that each can be changed during design or use without affecting the performance of the larger system. Structural wall and floor blanks, provided from wood product or light gauge steel manufacturers, are prepared – complete with fenestration, finishes, and pathways for all required wire, outlets, piping, ducts, fixture connections, etc. If selected as an option by the buyer, hydronic heat piping or high velocity forced air ducting is preinstalled in floor components. The modular components of an HVAC appliance in a compact, acoustically rated enclosure, configured to buyer specifications, are delivered to the integrator. The heating and cooling components are automatically sized using an algorithm that factors in the thermal properties of the enclosure, orientation, fenestration, etc. To increase energy efficiency, comfort, and health, the HVAC appliance and ductwork are located inside the insulated and air-sealed shell of the house. Available modules include domestic water heating, heating and cooling, air quality control (connected to wireless temperature, humidity, and particulate sensors), air filtration, energy recovery heat exchanger, humidification, kitchen and bathroom exhaust, clothes dryer exhaust, wireless remote control, and a single conduit to the exterior for the various vents and intakes.

4.3.4 Scenario: Installation-Part IV

An integrated utility supply core is installed on site during preparation of the foundation to accept the gas, electrical, communication, water supply, and waste connections from utility supply companies. Prefabricated structural wall, floor, and roof components arrive by truck at the site. These are nested for efficient transportation and are rapidly lifted into place by a crane. Preinstalled electrical and data wiring are typically connected in series at the interface of each structural component – terminating at the utility supply core. Non-structural infill walls and cabinetry – some with integrated lighting, data, and power – are connected to structural components. Satellite utility modules are pre-installed in wall components in the bathrooms and kitchen. Each contains water and gas supplies as required and is connected with a "home run" of flexible piping running through designated floor/wall pathways to the gas and water manifolds of the utility core. "Plug and Play" interoperable plumbing and lighting fixtures are then connected at each designated location. Wireless addressable lighting, HVAC, and communication control devices are installed as predetermined. (Their location and functionality can be rapidly reconfigured after move-in.) Utility pathways are accessible for ease of repair, alteration, and upgrade during occupancy.

4.4 Capturing the Value of Disentanglement

Barriers inherent to the structure of the current mass-produced housing industry make capturing the value of disentangling difficult. Companies will avoid investment in developing disentanglement implementation solutions and disentanglement will not take place as long as the individual players involved cannot capture value. The scenario exercise has laid out a hypothetical future that would allow the value of disentanglement to be captured. The factory-driven mass customization approach described provides enhanced value to customers through increased customization while avoiding the high costs often associated with additional design complexity. Utility disentanglement is a key part of avoiding the increase in costs generally associated with customization. The greatest need and opportunity for capturing the value of disentanglement is in this type of factory-based customized system. However, the hypothetical future presented requires some new elements be created in the home building industry: a network of manufacturers to develop high-value components and "builder/integrators" to assemble these components. These elements may be coming, but there must be a path from the current system to the desired future system. In the short term, systems could be pursued that capture the value of disentangling in the present, but are related to this future and may lead to it.

A good initial target for those interested in taking steps to reduce entanglement industry wide would be current factory-based customized construction with the goal of helping the industry reach the system presented in the scenario. Initially there will likely be few major manufacturers supplying the sort of complete walls and other high value components described in the scenario, so the builders/integrators in this segment will have to set up small factories (either individually or in collaboration). This is already the case for organizations like Bensonwood and Griffnerhaus described previously in this report. A more centralized process, such as that of Bensonwood and Griffnerhaus, allows for a more efficient incorporation of disentanglement because tasks normally performed by separate subcontractors, in heavily time-gated steps, can now be performed by a unified team. Team members work for either a single company or have long-term partnering arrangements. By controlling the building process to a greater degree, value can be obtained from changes to the process that might increase the cost of framing or finishing, but reduce the cost of utility installation and the overall time of construction. The following sections further examine how current builders can capture the value of disentangling. The value of disentangling utilities can be captured in two major areas, first during initial construction and then during renovation and repair.

4.4.1 Initial Construction

During initial construction, disentanglement solutions may require coordinating a change in the way two or more tasks are performed. For instance, use of a molding based raceway requires changes in the framing that will incur additional costs and changes in finishing that should not incur added costs, while considerably easing the installation of electrical wiring and plumbing. But if a separate subcontractor performs each of these tasks, the builder is unlikely to see all the potential benefits. Subcontractors respond to variations from the norm by increasing their bids and time required onsite, and it may take several bidding iterations for plumbers and electricians to lower their bids on jobs performed in systems with easier installation. There is little incentive for builders to change their way of doing things because they will bear the vast majority of the risk while most of the potential value will accrue to the subcontractors.

The solution to this problem is to increase the degree of cooperation among the various performers of tasks. Currently, subcontractors do not benefit monetarily by helping other subcontractors. They do the task for which they were hired in the way they know best. There is very little teamwork within the on-site subcontracted work environment, as each subcontractor generally strives to finish his piece of the job as quickly and cheaply as possible with little concern for the others who come after him. In the possible future scenario, manufacturers who create high-value components have replaced the subcontractor since these products do not require the sort of on-site work currently being performed by subcontractors. A minimally trained assembler could put together any of these high-value components without difficulty. However, until manufacturers are able to create products that simplify complex operations, other solutions must be pursued that create better coordination.

In the meantime, one way to improve coordination is to create partnerships among the different subcontractors and the builder, by developing a more extensive contract that shares risks and benefits more evenly. In practice, partnering in the residential home construction industry is difficult as it is antithetical to the current system organization, which emphasizes a strict division of labor. Negotiating contracts is expensive, and most are negotiated on a job-by-job basis. Contract negotiation adds to overhead costs. These costs may be justified if long-term partnering arrangements can be reached, but on a job-by-job basis such negotiations are likely still too expensive. Bensonwood and other panelized builders often employ this type of system: they do not hire utility installers in-house, as would a modular builder, but form long-term relationships to get value from the effort they put into training local subcontractors to work with their system. This works well for builders who operate repeatedly in the same localities, but is less useful for a builder who sells houses in many locations and therefore can't recoup training expenses. Any innovation in the system requires the retraining of a large number of local subcontractors. A potential solution to the training problem is to use the same utility installers and on-site assembly crews in all localities. This system would experience some of the same code variation and local inspection barriers that modular builders currently experience and are explained later in this section.

Another way to increase coordination among the various tasks would be to employ a subcontracting company that can perform all required types of utility installations. In this case, the risks and rewards are shared evenly, no contracts are required between various subcontractors, and one company controls all the utility installation. A variation on this concept is to simplify the work involved, then use "super-subs" that can perform a wide range of utility assembly tasks. Because the work has not yet been simplified, there are currently no super-subs, but as simplification occurs, such workers could easily develop within an organization that employs all types of utility installers as described above. These employees would learn to assemble the plumbing, electrical, and HVAC systems associated with a particular building system. Using one contractor for all utilities would vastly simplify the interactions and contracts required. Consolidating the trades and blurring the definitions of electrical, plumbing, and HVAC, contractors would improve coordination and eliminate time-gating of tasks. For this consolidation to be cost efficient, code updates might be needed to allow entry of new products that simplify work, such as PEX piping and quick-connect electrical plugs. Licensing updates would also be needed to create lower level licenses or certifications for specific skills or systems. It is currently too time consuming and costly for one person to become highly skilled and licensed in all trades. This could be feasible, however, if the super-sub only needed to train and receive certification in the simple standardized systems used in a specific type of home construction rather than in all types of electrical or plumbing systems. One possibility would be to have a licensed specialist for each utility system certify a part of the job, and handle any tricky situations that come up.

Modular and manufactured housing manufacturers use a system similar to having a single utility subcontractor. These manufacturers combine the work of mechanical, electrical and plumbing trades with framers, plasterers, and others by bringing everyone involved in the home's construction in-house, except possibly for those in charge of the final on-site placement and hookups. As a result, the contracting relationships for a modular or manufactured builder are much simpler. Each employee works for the manufacturers and may be required to perform many tasks. There are no contracts to be worked out when a change is made. The modular construction company bears all the risks and captures all the rewards, and thus reduces the uncertainty in decision making and the cost of negotiating contracts that share the risks and rewards. The findings of this project and of others reviewed suggest that moving more of the construction process off-site is the single most effective way of reducing the cost of housing. A factory-based custom approach combines this off-site building with an application in which disentangling can have the greatest impact, reducing the cost and complexity of custom solutions and capturing the maximum amount of initial construction value for all involved.

Some modular firms still must hire local subcontractors, due to local adoption and local interpretation of different versions or parts of the model code. Because of these code variations, a method of installing utilities that works well in one market may not pass inspection in another. Also, some utility connections must be made on site in homes constructed from more than one module. Even when local subcontractors make only a few of the final connections, they often carry the burden of responsibility for work conducted in the factory. Given the risk involved in taking responsibility for someone else's work, local contractors may charge as much for simply making a few final hookups as they would for doing the entire job. The builder thus pays for the utility installation twice, and all the cost benefits of efficiency gains are lost. Only HUD-code homes are exempt from this type of local inspection.

Complicated, prescriptive building codes and local interpretations can exacerbate the difficulty of introducing innovations, such as disentangled utility technologies. Local codes are perfectly acceptable when the builder is local, but can be problematic for factory-based builders that operate in many localities with a single set of utility installers. The success of a builder can depend on his relationship with the local inspectors, and an off-site builder does not generally have enough business in one locality to build this relationship. The cost and time required for an innovative product or method to be certified by the national ICC Evaluation Service and the issue of local code enforcement and adoption should all be examined further to understand how they may limit disentanglement innovation.

4.4.2 Code Changes

Codes can inhibit the adoption or development of innovations, such as those involved with disentanglement. One example of this has been experienced by Bensonwood Homes. Bensonwood uses quick-connect electrical connectors similar to those described in Section 4.5.6 in communities where allowed. But many communities do not allow these connectors. It would be unusual and expensive for a builder like Bensonwood to seek a national certification by the ICC Evaluation Service that could make obtaining variances easier or unnecessary altogether. The perceived market is probably not large enough for the manufacturer to seek the certification. It can be time consuming - and therefore expensive - to seek a code variance for products or methods without national certification. Even with such certification, local code bodies or inspectors are free to disallow an innovation with which they are unfamiliar. Bensonwood therefore simply chooses not to use disentangling technology, rather than go through the trouble of getting a variance. This situation limits efficiency by requiring factory-based builders to build to multiple standards, and may keep specific disentangling innovations out of the industry. Another example of codes inhibiting innovation is the creation of dedicated, accessible, open spaces between rooms and floors for utilities. This system is fundamental to open building and crucial to disentanglement, but presents a number of fire code incompatibilities that can prevent its introduction. For example, openings between rooms and floors are often required to be sealed, and access panels in walls, floors, and ceilings must provide fire separation, which can make them prohibitively expensive. The code and/or the local inspector are often not flexible enough to allow creative new solutions even if they provide the required safety, because they do not match what inspectors are used to seeing or the letter of the code.[31]

A performance-based national model code could allow innovative new solutions without the need for certification, but it would require local boards or inspectors to verify that products or methods are acceptable. Variance hearings and performance verification can be time-consuming for the board and the builder or manufacturer. Requiring all manufacturers and builders to spend the time and money on having their products and methods approved in the national model code would clearly slow innovation. One possibility is to develop guidelines to help educate the ICC

---

[31] Al Marzullo, TKG East Engineering, personal interview, January 2004.

on the value of disentanglement and advocate for some allowances for disentanglement solutions in the national model code. One possible area of code simplification would be to waive certain sections of the code if other precautions are taken. For example, homes with sprinkler systems could have an exemption from plugging holes in studs. Education efforts aimed at local inspectors and code bodies may also be necessary. Another possibility on the local side is to assign inspectors to work with specific factory builders, rather than by locality. These inspectors would perform inspections in the factory during construction and perform final on-site inspections wherever the home is built. Because the interstate commerce clause does not apply to housing other than HUD-code manufactured housing, a builder operating in multiple states would require a separate inspector for each state. In this way builders could limit the number of code versions, special allowances, and interpretations and - most importantly - build relationships with their inspectors in the same way that local subcontractors do.

An evaluation system could created which allows new innovations to be employed before they are incorporated in the national model code or obtain the market share necessary to fund full certification by the evaluation services. Another board in another location has already faced almost every code variance that is encountered by a local board, but little information is communicated between local boards. A searchable nationwide database of code variances that have been granted by local boards and substantiation for the approvals could be provided. When seeking a variance in a new locality, the builder and local code officials could use the national code registry to learn what other builders, product manufacturers, and regulatory boards have discovered in other localities. Changes in the code could then happen more quickly, as local boards would have easy access to precedent.

4.4.3 Renovation and Repair

The greatest benefit and improvement realized by disentangling utilities will come in easing renovation and repair. This can add tremendous value over the life of the home. Because the building will be easier to repair and upgrade - and will therefore last longer and be more functional throughout its life - the benefit to society is significant. Unfortunately, capturing this value during the initial construction and sale is nearly impossible in the current housing market. Most homeowners do not remain in a new home long enough to do major renovations. However, when that home is resold, there is a strong chance that the new owners will do some renovation to customize the space. In the current system, in which little value is placed on disentangled utilities, the benefits of disentanglement during renovation would potentially accrue to subsequent owners and the contractors/subcontractors hired for renovations. This is problematic, because they are not involved in the initial decision to implement disentanglement. It is clear that there is a mismatch of who must bear the cost and to whom the value created accrues.

A prescriptive method for dealing with this problem would be to simply incorporate disentangling into the building code. Similar to current code requirements that protect homeowners from improperly installed plumbing and ensure proper insulation, code requirements could be added to require proper allowance for repair and renovation of utilities over the life of the home. This type of concern for the life of building stock already receives great attention in Europe and may be worthy of consideration in the United States as well.

A less prescriptive approach would focus on creating market value from disentangling. However, it is difficult to clearly quantify how much value is created by the life-cycle benefits of disentanglement. The disentangled home should be worth more in resale because of its ease of renovation. In order to influence the new home building market, this value at resale would raise the price of the home in its initial sale. It may be possible for builders to educate their buyers about the value of easy renovations and the potential additional resale value, but this is not an activity most builders typically engage in, particularly development builders, so they may need assistance. One way to assist with the education process would be to create a new type of certification for homes being built with disentangled utilities, similar to the LEED certification for environmentally sustainable construction. Lending and governmental institutions could develop the details of this certification system.

Lenders could benefit considerably from homes built with disentangling in mind, because ease of renovation could figure positively into the resale value of the home, thereby reducing the potential risk of borrowers defaulting on loans. Even if a homeowner defaulted in the first year of the mortgage, the ability of the subsequent buyer to easily customize the home would increase its value in the foreclosure sale. Certified homes could be attractive to the market if buyers qualified for a rebate or lower finance rate. Similar rules could be adopted for federally subsidized housing programs, both single family government-backed mortgages, and multi-family housing projects.

Another way for builders to capture some of the societal benefit, which will accrue through the extended life and enhanced functionality of the home, is for Congress to create tax-breaks--similar to those for renewable energy generation--for homes built with disentangling technologies. The set of guidelines for certification could be created which describes the characteristics of a disentangled home that will allow it to be fully functional for many years. The guidelines could include a list of building technologies that meet certain standards and increase the life cycle value of the home. This set of characteristics and list of products and methods would provide guidance for lenders, new homebuyers, existing homeowners, builders, and manufacturers. It would inform the choice of building materials and components in the initial construction of the home, emphasize ease of repair and renovation, and provide a means of certifying these changes for purposes of assessing housing value. The market attractiveness of certified homes could be increased if government, public service, and awareness programs publicized their benefits.

4.5 Recommendations to Encourage Disentangled Home Systems

The following recommendations are offered for both near-term and longer-term future strategies to achieve an integrated "whole house" approach to disentangled utilities and the production of higher quality, more cost-effective, more responsive, and less energy consuming homes. These recommendations provide specific steps towards achieving the concepts of future home building described in the scenario presented earlier in this report. These recommendations follow from the research conducted to prepare this report and from a workshop held at TIAX in May 2004 with a small and varied group of building industry professionals. For more information on the workshop format and specific results, see Appendix D.

4.5.1 Builders as Integrators for Mass Customization

Motivation:
The baby boomers are significant purchasers of new housing in the United States and demand homes that meet their individual needs. Speaking at the 2002 Seniors Housing Symposium of the National Association of Home Builders, William Novelli, Executive Director and CEO of the American Association of Retired People, said the following about baby boomers:

> *"They love choice: set up the smorgasbord and let them help themselves. They will. They want information - and the more sources the better because they are not afraid to make decisions - but only on their own clock and in their own terms."*

Consumer companies are rapidly adapting their products to respond to the demands of this important market segment. Auto company websites encourage visitors to "build and price your car," and the companies are researching systems to make this marketing a practical service. Dell has become the most successful PC manufacturer by producing "batch orders of one" for individuals; the *New York Times* allows online members to "create a customized news alert" and Nokia offers interchangeable faceplates to personalize mobile phones. To be successful in this lucrative market segment, the housing industry must follow suit.

Promising Current Solution Efforts:
Large merchant builders are beginning to offer buyers customization services, but the choices are mostly cosmetic and limited to those options that are largely disconnected from the generic building shell. Smaller, innovative builders are developing strategies for delivering substantial customization – from form to finishes.

GriffnerHaus, a prefabricated custom homebuilder based in Austria, is now developing a second generation of prefabrication technology – moving towards almost entirely automated fabrication of building envelope structural components. It has developed prototype wall panels that can be custom fabricated, with integrated space for hydronic-heating pipes. A subsidiary company, Systemacasa, has developed "Virtual Architect" to allow customers to configure a custom design online.

Design visualization room, CNC milling machines for prefabricated panels, and a completed GriffnerHaus home. [32]
Figure 17: GriffnerHaus, Austria

---

[32] http://www.giffnerhomes.com/

Bensonwood Homes, a prefabricated custom homebuilder based in New Hampshire, is one of the U.S. leaders in the application of new design and fabrication technologies to housing. Key to improving the efficiency of its production process is the disentanglement of utilities and the availability of new MEP systems, now emerging in Europe and Asia. The company uses some of these innovative systems, but many of them are difficult to obtain for the U.S. market, or are not allowed by code. (More information on Bensonwood practices can be found in Appendix C.)

 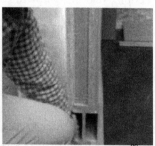 

Panelized home under construction, panel with integrated utility raceway.[33]
Figure 18: Bensonwood, New Hampshire

Customized prefabricated house construction has the potential to become increasingly important for the following reasons:

- Emerging technologies for disentangled plumbing, electrical, and HVAC systems are more readily justified in a prefabricated component approach in which additional costs are offset by labor saving, efficient production.
- Prefabrication addresses site-based quality control and labor shortage issues.
- An integrated design, fabrication, and supply-chain management system can enable a workable strategy for creating personalized homes.
- Better design and engineering, and tighter tolerances in production, can improve quality and occupant comfort.
- U.S. and European manufacturers of commodity building materials are looking to migrate towards high-value systems and components to create new markets, increase profits, and respond to foreign competition.
- CAD-CAM systems for efficient fabrication are becoming cost effective for smaller operations.

Next Steps:
The first step should be the creation of a consortium representing all major stakeholders to develop a high-level "system architecture" for mass customized homes that takes advantage of emerging design and fabrication technologies. Widespread adoption of better methods of design and construction clearly depends on establishing the "system architecture" of the home. Manufacturers, designers, engineers, and subcontractors can contribute to this effort, but builders who are willing to become real system integrators can best accomplish it. To achieve economies of scale and reduce costs below that of conventional framing, open standards must be developed for structural and infill wall and floor elements. These standards should delineate connections

---

[33] http://www.bensonwood.com/

and pathways for utilities. Standards will allow manufacturers to make standardized components for use by all builders, instead of a number of incompatible proprietary systems.

4.5.2   Building Objects and Software

Motivation:
Efficient design, coordination, and prefabrication of building components for custom housing will ultimately draw upon the product libraries provided by each manufacturer, with standardized digital descriptions so that elements can be used directly by computation design and manufacturing systems.

Promising Current Solution Efforts:
The International Alliance for Interoperability (IAI) has proposed "Industry Foundation Classes" (IFC) to specify how "things" found in construction (components such as toilets, sinks, windows, etc.) can be electronically represented on a computer. These specifications represent a data structure on which the electronic representation of a building project, needed for the exchange of data between software applications, is based. The first phase of the IFC development process is nearing completion and commercial CAD applications, such as AutoDesk's Architectural Desktop and MicroStation Tri Forma, now conform to this standard. Several producers of more specialized software for the building and construction industry are also working with the IFC system. As part of this effort, aecXML has been developed to facilitate the exchange of architectural, engineering, and construction (AEC) data on the Internet. (XML refers to a type of structured text data called "eXtensible Markup Language.") This work is being lead by Bentley Systems, the leader of CAD software for large AEC firms; and John Marshall, Vice President, Product Development for McGraw-Hill Construction, and Chairman of the aecXML Domain.

If adopted by manufacturers, this approach should allow a particular window model to be inserted directly into 2D plans, 2D elevations, and 3D models with standardized conventions for delineating rough openings, reference points, costs, etc. It should also enable the automatic routing of plumbing and wiring given predetermined raceways and connection locations.

Other industries have successfully implemented an analogous process. In the domain of electronics design, Simulation Program with Integrated Circuit Emphasis (SPICE) began in the early 1970s as a stand-alone program. It has evolved to use standard formats to describe the properties and performance of electronic components. A wide range of software exists--from simple and free to complex and costly--that use these models. Most major component manufacturers provide SPICE models of their products for use in the simulation and design process for electronic circuits. Protel is a CAD tool for the design and fabrication of electronic circuits that has the capacity to use SPICE models in simulations. In designing circuit layout, it can automatically determine the appropriate route for a trace on the printed circuit board for fabrication. The "wiring" is determined automatically.

The development of a standard description of objects on the Internet, if combined with industry standards for connections among components, may enable unprecedented improvements in the quality and efficiency of house design, fabrication, and construction. Technologies exist in other industries that could be applied to housing.

Next Steps:

For residential construction, the development of standard methods of describing building components should be initiated as a joint effort of builders/integrators, manufacturers, and AEC software companies. Work is needed on aecXML and other efforts to make a more optimal software representation. Next steps should include the creation of a working group representing all three stakeholders to interface with the IAI and participate in related efforts. HUD could facilitate this important work through funding, coordination, and support.

4.5.3 Separate Building Layers and Decoupled Spaces for Utilities

Motivation:

Most new homes are largely entangled systems. Their design does not acknowledge that each system has a different useful lifespan. Systems with longer lifetimes often encapsulate short lifetime components, which makes the latter's replacement difficult. The challenge in a new model for housing production is to achieve functional integration of components, while maintaining physical independence and ensuring design flexibility and ease of access, repair, and replacement.

More specifically, the home must be separated into independent layers according to the useful life expectancy: structural elements may last from 50 to many hundreds of years; the exterior finishes and roof from 20 to 40 years; pipes, wire, and ducts from 15 to 20 years; appliances up to 10 years; and processors and sensors up to 5 years.

Promising Current Solution Efforts:

SIPS (Structural Insulated Panel System) are a type of building panel for floors, walls and roofs in residential and commercial buildings. SIPS are typically made using expanded polystyrene (EPS), or polyisocyanurate rigid foam insulation, sandwiched between two structural skins of oriented strand board (OSB). Wiring may be pulled through panels in preformed "chases" or channels built into the foam. Electricians use a fish tape and feed the wires through panel chases without compressing insulation or drilling through studs, as is common in stick-built construction. Plumbing is typically installed in interior walls and floors, but not in exterior walls. Where exterior wall vent pipes are necessary, chases can be formed in the foam cores. Access is typically not possible after construction.

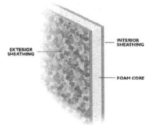

Figure 19: SIPS Panel: Layers of Materials

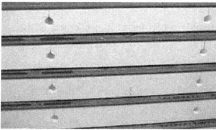

Figure 20: SIPS Panel: Wiring Chases

SIPS are a useful first step in the development of high performance wall, floor, and roof components. They are largely designed to replace standard stick-built frame construction – not to serve as an agile system for future mass customization.[34]

Bensonwood Homes has created accessible raceways in prefabricated wall and ceiling systems for routing wires, pipes, and ducts. Bensonwood currently does not use prefabricated panels for structure, but is exploring this possibility. Floor trusses can also provide a significant space for utilities and, when used in conjunction with removable floor or ceiling panels, can provide access to utilities. As experience with these concepts grows, builders will take advantage of them to increase disentanglement.

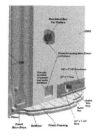  

Utility pathways in wall panels and timber frame with accessible ceiling.[35]
Figure 21: Bensonwood Homes Accessible Raceway

Next Steps:
Next steps could include the collaboration of a dedicated group representing large wood product companies, SIPA, manufacturers of electrical and plumbing components, and builders/integrators to develop more sophisticated approaches to prefabricated floor, wall, and roof components that provide fully accessible utility raceways. Wood product companies, such as International Paper, Boise Cascade, MeadWestvaco, Huber, and Weyerhaeuser, as well as companies currently producing SIPS panels, should be invited to participate in efforts to expand the use of energy efficient SIPS, and to develop criteria for next-generation wall, floor, and roof panels that provide a predefined, decoupled, accessible space for utilities. While these advanced systems are being developed and gaining market share, interim methods could be developed for builders using traditional stud framing. An example would be to create a decoupled space for utilities by

---

[34] http://www.sips.org/what_are_sips/what_are_sips.html
   http://sips.org/what_are_sips/electric_plumbing.html
   http://www.sips.org/technical/wiring.html
[35] http://www.bensonwood.com

precutting a narrow trough into studs and covering this "raceway" with removable crown molding or baseboards. A quantitative analysis of the cost and time reductions in utility installation should be performed for each existing and future decoupled space technology.

4.5.4 Integrated Utility Gateway Module

Motivation:
There is currently no coordinated interface among the exterior gas, water, waste, power, telephone, and cable services and the house. Utilities typically enter the house at a point that each trade finds convenient for its individual operation. This often results in inefficient use of space – with wires and pipes fully entangled in the structure. It makes service and repair difficult, disruptive, and often more expensive than necessary.

Promising Current Solution Efforts:
Since the building industry is based on a division of labor by trade, with separate contracts executed for installation of plumbing, electrical, cable, and telephone service, there is little incentive to coordinate. Utility companies are also typically independent entities with their own work practices and labor force. As a result, industry is currently expending little effort to develop integrated and coordinated approaches for ways the best ways utilities can be configured to enter a house.

Next Steps:
One potential method is to make a single large trench, with a conduit separator laid in the bottom that has space for each utility coming into the home and a single connection panel for all the services coming into the home. The trench is kept open as part of the initial site-work and the utilities are laid in as the various utility companies install them. The trench is filled in before final landscaping. There are advantages in having only one trench, one connection area, and one area for penetrations through the home. However, there are also potential safety and regulatory issues. As utility companies merge and trades consolidate, Federal, state, and local governments could support the development of a single utility gateway module.

4.5.5 Integrated "Satellite" Utility Modules

Motivation:
There are a limited number of points in a home with intensive connections to utilities: kitchens, bathrooms, and laundry areas. This situation offers opportunities for a coordinated and laborsaving approach to connecting fixtures and appliances to utilities – and one that promotes disentanglement.

Promising Current Solution Efforts:
Industry and academic researchers have engaged in a number of ambitious projects to prefabricate units that integrate the complex water supply, waste water, and venting required in bathrooms – allowing for rapid connection to utilities and rapid and accurate attachment of sinks, toilets, tubs, and showers. Several companies have developed products that could evolve into integrated satellite utility modules.

Figure 22: Quickframe Prefabricated Plumbing Wall by IPPEC (UK)

In these systems, all services are housed in a prefabricated plumbing wall. Fixtures may be attached on either side of that wall. One commercial concept includes universal connections to sink and shower mixers, and allows attachment of wall-hung toilets. The shower partition wall can encase the entire waste and rising mains pipe. Access to the PEX pipe distribution manifold is located in the frames.[36] A major advantage to this system is that it could enable further production efficiencies in the factory environment.

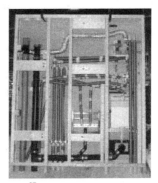

All pipes and wires are concentrated in one central installation module.[37]
Figure 23: Integrated Single-Family House Utility Wall Prototype

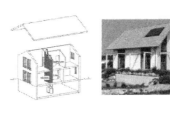

Figure 24: Integrated Multi-Story Utility Wall Prototype[38]

Next Steps:
Plumbers and plumbing component manufacturers could focus on reaching common performance standards for advanced plumbing components to maximize interchangeability,

---

[36] www.ippec.co.uk

[37] Collaboration between the Fachhochschule Rosenheim (University of Applied Science), house manufacturers and the installation supplying industries, and built by 'Regnauer Fertigbau GmbH & CO KG', a manufacturer for prefabricated buildings.

[38] Fachhochschule and 'Regnauer Fertigbau GmbH & CO KG'

minimize retraining, and thus maximize the market. This could be accomplished under the auspices of professional and trade associations with HUD encouragement and support. Module design could be standardized using these specifications to provide enhanced access and disentanglement.

4.5.6   Electrical Distribution Systems and Fixtures

Motivation:
Conventional electrical system installation includes tasks such as cutting cable to length, stripping the insulation, making the terminal connections in junction boxes, and hard wiring fixtures. While materials are inexpensive, field labor is expensive and varies in quality. There is no *technical* barrier to implementing a modular electrical system in a house. Implementation would save installation time and labor. Repair would be simplified, allowing some level of modification to be done by the homeowner.

Promising Current Solution Efforts:
Power distribution in airplanes, automobiles, and computers, on the other hand, uses prefabricated wiring harnesses and modular connectors. Current CAD programs, now widely used in other, non-housing industries, can generate a bill of materials for MEP systems. Companies, such as A.& H. Meyer and Wieland, offer modular "plug and play" electrical components that are widely used in Europe. Some components have UL ratings for use in the United States. However, code approvals and the general reluctance of the trades to innovate have slowed implementation.

The ST18 connector system and the GST18 system, which are standardized in some countries.[39]
Figure 25: Modular Electrical Connectors

---

[39] A. & H. Meyer, Germany (http://www.ah-meyer.de/)

Figure 26: Wieland Gesis Electrical System Diagram[40]

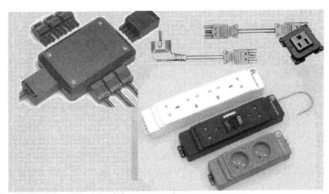

Figure 27: Wieland Gesis Modular Electrical Components

Next Steps:
Builders/integrators, electrical-component manufacturers, progressive electrical contractors, and AEC software companies should collaborate in a concentrated effort to develop non-proprietary connections and design/specification software for modular electrical systems. Their goal should be to save design and wiring time, without increasing materials costs and while maintaining error rates close to zero. Connection systems should be developed that allow components to connect to current wiring, as well as to other system components. Codes must be updated to allow widespread adoption of modular plug electrical systems.

4.5.7 Distributed Energy Production & Building Integrated PVs

Motivation:
As discussed previously, history has shown that adding new systems to the home has typically led to further utility entanglement. Therefore, continued progress towards disentanglement in the future could remain a major challenge as home systems become more complex. For example, distributed energy systems represent one possible future addition to the home. Distributed energy generation may represent the wave of the future in energy production. Distribution costs make up a large portion of the total cost of electricity delivered to most homes. Expanding the nation's transmission and distribution infrastructure is also problematic. Government incentives for installing distributed renewable energy, especially photovoltaic solar (PV), have increased in

---

[40] http://www.gesis.com/

recent years, especially with the introduction of Zero Energy Homes (ZEH). The costs of PV components have come down considerably in the last few decades, and an increase in production volume is forecast to continue. However, PV and other components increase entanglement. Problems (such as leaks) and the added costs associated with building penetrations to accommodate solar collectors are major barriers to increased market penetration of ZEH.

Promising Current Solution Efforts:
Multiple innovators in the solar industry are looking for ways to integrate solar systems into existing building skin components. Thin-film solar PV cells can be applied to a wide variety of substrates in process-type continuous fabrication plants. Integrating PV into weatherproof skin components lowers the cost of PV equipment and installation due to lower overall material costs and the fact that only one layer needs to be installed. PV may be integrated into asphalt shingles, metal roofing, or plastic siding, using the weatherproof layer as a substrate, with manufactured standardized penetrations of the weatherproof layer to allow electricity into the home. Alternatively, existing PV panels may be used as shading devices (awnings). The transparent outer part of most PV modules, which acts as a weatherproof layer, could be integrated into roof components. Instead of having weatherproof PV modules, a transparent roof of acrylic or glass could be built, and solar cells could be mounted in frames attached to the underside of the roof, creating PV macro-modules that provide the same functions as roof panels in a panelized building system. This could significantly lower the cost of the solar components and avoid penetrations in the roof. The same transparent roof system could be used with solar thermal technology or for de-lighting applications. These roof panels could be built with standardized electrical connections for PV and water connections for solar thermal.

Next Steps:
Further research should be conducted to determine the feasibility of various strategies for transmitting solar energy through the weatherproof layer of the home and integrating solar components into building components. A building industry ZEH standards group, in consultation with the solar industry and interested government agencies (such as Department of Energy (DOE), HUD, and California Energy Commission (CEC)) could develop standards for PV and solar thermal penetrations and module connections. These standards could cover both integrated weatherproof solar modules (solar components on the inside of transparent weatherproof layers) and thin-film solar weatherproofing materials (thin-film PV on the outside of weatherproof substrates – shingles, siding, etc.). With these guidelines in place, new products could be designed to reflect disentangling needs and make rethinking/retrofit unnecessary.

4.5.8 Plumbing Systems and Fixtures

Motivation:
Water supply piping for new home construction in the United States is typically plastic PVC pipe, field cut and glued, or copper pipe, field cut and soldered. As with electrical work, materials are inexpensive. Field labor is expensive and varies in quality. Entangled systems are commonplace, and repair and replacement is difficult. Plumbing systems that reduce complexity and field labor are more common in Europe and Asia than in the United States.

Promising Current Solution Efforts:

PEX (cross-linked polyethylene) piping is readily becoming the standard hot and cold water supply in Europe, and its use is increasing in the United States. Its flexibility and strength at temperatures ranging from below freezing to 200 degrees Fahrenheit make it appropriate for hot and cold water plumbing systems and hydronic radiant heating systems. The advantages of PEX piping include its ability to withstand high temperature and pressure, resistance to corrosion and scale, frost-free and noise-free attributes, hygienic material, and sealed ring systems. Flexible in-floor piping, which does not require joints to turn corners, reduces maintenance costs and condensation from cold pipes. It requires no soldering, bending, or threading tools. A wide variety of fittings and manifolds allows for agile design. The flexibility of PEX makes it appropriate to run through the utility pathways of prefabricated wall and floor components.

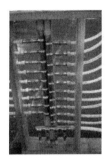  

Plumbing manifolds and schematic hot and cold water supply installation – Aquapex PEX system.[41]
Figure 28: Plumbing Supply System, Uponor Wirsbo

Many companies also make proprietary systems that bring together the benefits of rigid copper pipe and flexible plastic pipe. For example, the Geberit Mepla system consists of a highly flexible pipe connected by PVDF or brass fittings, using a crimping process that ensures a leak-proof seal. The pipe can be bent, by hand or by tool, into any position, which it then is able to maintain, unlike plastic piping systems, through an inner aluminum layer. This system has been used in Europe for over 12 years.

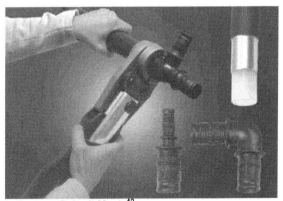

Figure 29: Plumbing Supply System, Geberit Mepla[42]

---

[41] http://www.wirsbo.com/
[42] http://www.us.geberit.com/

Next Steps:
Building codes should be updated to allow the use of novel plumbing systems that have been proven to perform well in the home. HUD could perform a study of the potential benefits of using simplified plumbing connections, in cooperation with relevant regulatory authorities and industry groups. Plumbing should be redesigned for incorporation into raceways and other decoupled space designs to achieve significant disentangling in future construction. Such changes offer a high potential payoff for HUD in promoting affordability and reduced lifecycle cost.

4.5.9 Modular HVAC Systems

Motivation:
Conversations with developers and contractors point to HVAC systems as perhaps the most problematic aspect of the design and construction process – and the source of a large number of occupant complaints. Many argue that industry does not provide products that meet the needs of a modern, energy efficient apartment building or highly insulated single-family house. A complete integrated system is needed that has one-point responsibility, is installed with little skilled field labor, and requires little or no site engineering. Typical forced air systems often fail to meet customer expectations because they require a large amount of space, engineering, and architectural design. These systems are also one of the largest contributors to entanglement.

Promising Current Solution Efforts:
Many commercial systems address some of these concerns, but overall responsibility still tends to be unclear and these products are generally sold as components rather than complete systems. Mini-split units, popular in Asia, offer a system approach to air-conditioning that provides efficient multi-zone control. Rather than move cold air through ducts from a central coil, a mini-split supplies refrigerant through small tubing to individual fan-coil units in each room. Another option is the "Unichiller" manufactured by Unico, which is similar to a mini-split system, but distributes cold water rather than refrigerant. For heating, these systems are generally combined with a hydronic (hot water) system, an electric coil, or a heat pump. System improvement could include combining a chilled water and hydronic heating system to share the distribution network, as is done in many commercial installations. Typical central-forced air systems can also be replaced by high-velocity systems that distribute air through flexible, pre-insulated 2" (inner diameter) tubing that slides easily through wall structures and around obstructions.

Next Steps:
Next steps could include assembling DOE (as lead), HUD, trade associations, builders/integrators, HVAC engineers, equipment manufacturers, and other government agencies, such as NIST to define the design criteria for improved systems that meet the above criteria. This task force could accelerate commercialization of advanced systems by addressing the following questions: How small can the components be? What range of loads should be assumed? How much modularity is prudent? What flows can be integrated? (For example, can the combustion gases from the water heater be run though the heat exchanger?) Can kitchen and bath exhaust be integrated? One promising possibility is to create a modular HVAC "appliance" that would provide efficient multi-zone control with almost no distribution, while also reducing space requirements and bringing the current separately engineered systems under one single point of engineering responsibility. It would include:

- Domestic hot water heating and cooling (for cooling coil)
- Air quality sensing
- Air filtration
- Heat exchange
- Humidification
- Kitchen and bathroom exhaust fans
- Distributed wireless control
- Single grill assembly to the exterior for the various vents and intakes

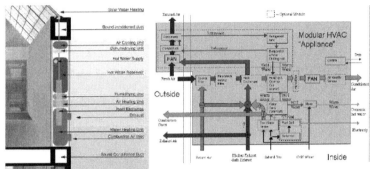

Figure 30: Schematic Modular HVAC Appliance[43]

The modular components would be enclosed in a compact, acoustically/rated enclosure with a single penetration to the exterior for the various vents and intakes. The components could stack vertically to use a minimum of floor space. The reduced engineering, installation, and servicing costs, as well as the reduced floor space dedicated to HVAC and the performance and health benefits of a properly engineered system could make a more expensive unit justifiable to developers.

4.5.10 Sensors and Control Devices: Low Bandwidth Data

Motivation:
Typical home systems use simple on/off 120V AC for lighting control and multiple conductor on/off 24V AC for HVAC control. These two systems work in essentially the same way, just as a light turns on when the circuit connects with the switch, so does the heat turn on when the thermostat connects the "heating" wire. If the "cooling" wire is connected instead, the air conditioning system will turn on. These low-tech systems for transferring low-bandwidth data have advantages, but also limitations. There is increasing demand for new data transfer systems for lighting control, energy management, HVAC control, security, and other sensor and control systems. Currently each of these new control systems uses a unique proprietary system and requires its own wiring and hardware. A common sensing and control infrastructure would minimize duplication, increase performance, and reduce costs. Addressable lighting and HVAC control systems (in which each device has an IP address) would eliminate the need to physically

---

[43] MIT House_n Research Group

connect the device directly to the controller, and would allow, for example, light switches to be assigned to light fixtures after construction without making any wiring changes.

Promising Current Solution Efforts:
Existing control systems for lighting, HVAC, etc., are almost exclusively proprietary and usually address only a single application. Lightolier (Compse PLC), Lutron (Homeworks), and others have developed addressable lighting control systems that streamline the task of assigning switches or occupancy sensors to light fixtures. The Digital Addressable Lighting Interface (DALI) protocol has been created to bring together some of these proprietary systems, but no addressable lighting protocol has been widely adopted.[44] Advanced HVAC control will require additional data distribution, and systems for preventative health and aging in place will become more cost effective if industry adopts open standards for low-bandwidth communications.

A variety of emerging technologies could dramatically improve the effectiveness, agility, and cost effectiveness of control systems. Simple two-wire low-voltage systems, power line carrier systems, low-cost alternatives that piggy back on existing high-bandwidth systems, and low-cost low-bandwidth wireless are some areas where progress is being made. The Responsive Environments Groups at the MIT Media Lab, for example, has developed a wireless, self-powered pushbutton device that could be developed into a "stick-on" light switch. Without attached wires or battery, this technology could enable occupants to locate switches and assign control wherever desired.

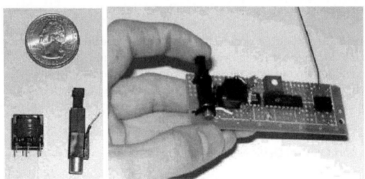

Figure 31: Self-Powered, Wireless Pushbutton Controller [45]

Next Steps:
Next steps could include the formation of a government-sponsored working group to define design criteria for next-generation residential building control systems and to help coordinate efforts at creating open standards for building control systems that remove proprietary barriers to growth. DALI efforts should be expanded to include other data and electrical communication needs as well, such as sensor networks. Sensor networks may be used for security and HVAC systems and may someday be used to maintain and monitor health and well being in the home.

---

[44] http://www.dali-ag.org/
[45] Joseph A. Paradiso and Mark Feldmeier, Responsive Environments Group, MIT Media Lab.
http://www.media.mit.edu/resenv/pubs/papers/UbiComp-Switch-submitted.pdf

5   Conclusions

The history of home building has seen the addition of new utilities and significant increases in the distribution and quantity of existing utilities to meet the demands of increasingly complex activities and appliances. This proliferation and expansion has led to entanglement. It appears this trend will continue in the future, with the addition of distributed home energy systems and other technologies, and through increasing demand for customization in housing. Some products to alleviate entanglement have been developed, but have experienced limited market penetration to date, due to structural and commercial barriers within the current housing industry and because the products have not been part of an integrated whole-house solution. Solutions are difficult to implement due to the fragmented nature of the industry. Sharing risks and benefits across multiple entities adds significant contractual expense. Factory-based construction can consolidate multiple businesses operations into one, thereby reducing contracting costs and unifying risk and benefit. However, local building codes can discourage off-site work by forcing the local contractors who make the final connections to be fully responsible for the factory-installed system; therefore, forcing them to charge a risk premium that negates the efficiency that would be gained from installing the utilities in the factory. Another factor limiting innovation is a requirement for builders to adapt construction techniques to meet diverse local codes and interpretations, which reduces efficiency for builders trying to apply innovative solutions, particularly "whole house" solutions. Unfortunately, obtaining building code approval for innovative products and methods can be even more costly and time consuming than adapting and using local subcontractors (see Sections 4.4.1 and 4.4.2 for more detail). The combination of these factors often results in the status quo being the most business-efficient (or profitable) choice, even when it is not the most technically efficient or the most affordable for the customer in the long run.

Solutions for disentangling utilities must be tailored to the market in which they will be used. The local market topography (average cost, code requirements, popularity of "do-it-yourself") and the builder's business model (site-based vs. factory-based, custom vs. generic) must be considered when introducing new products for the purposes of disentangling. Factory-based custom builders, especially in markets with higher than average cost, flexible code requirements, and a proclivity for do-it-yourself home maintenance, offer the greatest potential for capturing value from disentangling utilities. Early efforts should therefore focus on factory-based custom builders, with the goal of expanding market share through education, marketing, code improvements, etc. Later, ideas can be transferred into other markets as undertaking disentangling efforts becomes acceptable (and profitable) for builders in those markets.

Disentangling utilities is very important to factory-based custom builders, because it reduces the complexity of system interactions and the cost of customization. Disentangling and use of components with standardized connections allows components to be used interchangeably. A component can be anything from a sink assembly to a whole kitchen, as long as the connections are standardized so that changing a single item won't affect the rest of the design. The use of a factory-based process allows the builder to capture the value of disentangling utilities. This is crucial, because it is generally the builder who assumes the risk for modifying the system and training the utility installers. Because control is more centralized, there is greater potential to adapt to new technologies quickly, as long as standard component connections are maintained.

Two hurdles to overcome are the difficulties in getting code approvals and the lack of inexpensive building components with standard connections. Government/industry working groups should be formed to develop strategies for modifying building codes and build upon existing products to develop component standards to encourage disentanglement. If these issues are overcome, factory-based custom builders will be able to capture value from disentangling during initial home construction. Those who use disentangled methods will have a competitive advantage.

Another major area of value from disentanglement is lifecycle cost reductions: home maintenance, renovation, and repair. Unfortunately, it is difficult for the builder to capture this value when the home is built, because the home buyer will likely not see the potential for future benefit. Therefore, lifecycle benefits will not increase the financial benefit that a builder can achieve by disentangling, unless the buyer can be educated or other incentives are created. Any reduction in lifecycle costs, increase in the lifetime of homes, or increase in the quality of older homes enhances the long-term value and supply of affordable housing and benefits society. As such, it may be reasonable for disentangling to be incentivized by lenders or government agencies.

While disentanglement has great potential to reduce the time, cost, and complexity of initial construction, it must first be applied to markets and building methods in which it can have the greatest benefit. Institutional barriers in codes and trade restrictions must be eliminated to allow these building methods to be profitable and the benefit to be realized. A greater degree of customization in residential construction will become affordable if it is accompanied by disentanglement to reduce the complexity of customization. Technologies, construction methods, and institutional advances that make utilities decoupled and accessible will also reduce the lifecycle costs of homeownership, but these improvements may need to be incentivized to find widespread use. HUD should consider ways to encourage developments towards this goal as part of its overall mission to make housing better and more affordable.

Appendix A: Research Methodology

A literature search was conducted including printed journals, both domestic and foreign, searching the web, interviewing building industry professionals, and attending the International Builders Show. The literature search was intended to discover how homes became entangled, past and current efforts at disentangling, both in the US and abroad, and the characteristics of different building systems in use today as well as to develop a database of building component technologies that might be used in solving the problem of entanglement.

The next step was to establish the relationships among different parts of the process. This included understanding the physical relationship of utilities to other parts of the home, the way in which installation work is performed, and the relationship among different participants in the construction of a home. The impacts of these relationships with utility entanglement and possible disentanglement were evaluated.

Solutions and future strategies were then developed. A workshop with building industry professionals was held to provide critical evaluation and input to our solution strategies. Barriers to solutions were examined, and strategies adjusted accordingly. A coherent vision of the future of housing, including disentangled utilities was forecast, and strategies for solving the problems in making this future a reality were outlined. Real world physical solutions were developed, in addition to strategies for capturing the value of disentangled utilities, and methods for overcoming institutional barriers to possible solutions.

Appendix B
Component/Product List

Device	Category	Utility	Manufacturer(s)	Disentanglement	Webpage
DALI (Digital Addressable Lighting Interface	Addressable Lighting	Electrical	Members include: ERCO, Johnson Controls, Lightolier, Lutron, Luxmate, Philips Lighting, Troll, Universal Lighting Technologies	Reduces size, Eliminates Utilities	http://www.dali-ag.org/
High velocity mini-duct systems	Ducts	HVAC	Unico, Inc.	Reduces size	
Removable Flooring (Rug squares)	Finish	Structure	Legaqto Carpet System by Milliken	Improves Accessibility	www.legatocarpet.com
Crimpsert Plumbing Fittings for Flexible Pipe	Fittings	Plumbing	Vanguard	Eases Installation	www.vaguardpipe.com
Pushfit plumbing connections	Fittings	Plumbing	John Guest, IBP Ltd.	Eases Installation	http://www.johnguest.com/http://www.screwfix.com/app/sfd/cat/cat.jsp?cld=101595
Dryer hose cavity	Fittings	HVAC	Dryerbox	Eases Installation, Reduces Size	www.dryerbox.com
Waterless or Composting Toilet	Fixture	Plumbing	Envirolet	Eliminates Utilities	http://store.yahoo.com/sacor/index.html
Flexible Water Piping	Pipe	Plumbing	Vanguard	Improves Flexibility	www.vanguardpipe.com
Flexible Gas	Pipe	Gas	Gaslite	Improves Flexibility	www.gaslite.com
Ducted Skylight	Pipe	Light	ODL Tubular skylight	Eliminates Utilities	www.odl.com
Flexible Water	Pipe	Plumbing	Plub-pex, RTI Pex Piping systems	Improves Flexibility	www.rtisystems.com
Flexible Water	Pipe	Plumbing	REHAU	Improves Flexibility	www.REHAU-NA/.com
Flexible Water	Pipe	Plumbing	Wirsbo	Improves Flexibility	www.wirsbo.com
Flexible Water	Pipe	Plumbing	ZURIN	Improves Flexibility	www.zum.com
Flexible Water	Pipe	Plumbing	IPEX	Improves Flexibility	www.ipexinc.com
CPVC Water	Pipe	Plumbing	Flowguard gold	Eases Installation	www.flowguardgold.com
CPVC Water	Pipe	Plumbing	EverTuff, Coastline Plastics LLC, Vitaculic	Eases Installation	www.flowguardgold.com
Flexible Plumbing, Fittings and Foam Floor Tiles	Pipe, Fittings	Plumbing, Gas	GE (from GE Plastic House)	Improves Flexibility, Organizes Utilities, Eases Installation	Flexibility, Organization, Installation
Power Connectors	Plugs	Electrical	Anderson Power Products	Eases Installation	http://www.andersonpower.com/
Raceway Systems	Raceway	Electrical	Wiremold	Organizes Utilities, Improves Accessibility	www.wiremold.com
Raceway Baseboard in-wall	Raceway	Structure	Benson Homes	Improves Accessibility Adds space for utilities	www.bensonwood.com
Wire trough	Raceway	Electrical, Data	Carlon	Organizes Utilities, Improves Accessibility	www.carlon.com
Flexible conduit for wiring	Raceway	Electrical, Data	Carlon	Organizes Utilities	www.carlon.com
Polytrak raceway	Raceway	Electrical, Data	Hubbell	Organizes Utilities	www.hubbell-wiring.com

Device	Category	Utility	Manufacturer(s)	Disentanglement	Webpage
Molded Architectural Baseboard Raceway	Raceway	Electrical, Data	GE (part of GE Plastics House)	Organizes Utilities, Improves Accessibility	
Flexible plastic conduit and baseboard raceways	Raceway	Electrical	Carlon-conduit, Wiretracks-raceway	Organizes Utilities, Improves Accessibility, Improves Flexibility	http://www.hometech.com/techwire/resigard.html
Raceway Systems	Raceway	Electrical	Wiretracks	Organizes Utilities	www.wiretracks.com
Pipe and Electrical Support Systems	Supports	Plumbing, HVAC	Erico	Organizes Utilities	www.erico.com
Pre-Cast Concrete Structure	Supports	Structure	Br. Mike Wilmot, SJ	Organizes Utilities, Eases Installation	
Open Truss Joist	Supports	Structure	SpaceJoist	Adds space for Utilities	www.spacejoist.com
Open Truss Joist	Supports	Structure	TrimJoist	Adds space for Utilities	www.trimjoist.com
Open Truss Joist	Supports	Structure	Joist-rite, Marinoware	Adds space for Utilities	www.marinoware.com
Open Truss Joist	Supports	Structure	TrussFrames	Adds space for Utilities	www.trussframe.com
Steel Framing	Supports	Structure	FrameMax	Adds Space for Utilities	www.framemax.com
SIPS panels	Supports	Structure	Pacemaker	Eases Installation, Organizes Utilities	www.buildsips.com
SIPS panels	Supports	Structure	SolidCore, EPS	Eases Installation, Organizes Utilities	www.epsbuildings.com
Insulated Concrete Forms (interior forms)	Supports	Structure	Hadrian Tridi-systems	Eases Installation	www.tridipanel.com
Insulated Concrete Forms	Supports	Structure	Eco-Block	Eases Installation, Organizes Utilities	www.eco-block.com
Insulated Concrete Forms	Supports	Structure	Royal Building Systems	Eases Installation	www.rbsdirect.com
Electrical installation tools	Tool	Electrical	Rack-a-tiers	Eases Installation	www.rack-a-tiers.com
Power and Data Busways	Wire	Electrical	EuTrac, Universal Electric (Starline)	Organizes Utilities	
Structured Wire	Wire	Electrical	Belden	Organizes Utilities	http://store.yahoo.com/broadbandutopia/composite.html
Wireless data	Wire	Data	Intel	Eliminates Utilities	http://www.intel.com/
Powerline Data Carrier	Wire	Data	Intellon, Phonex Broadband Corp	Eliminates Utilities	http://www.intellon.com/ http://www.phonex.com/
Single shared network	Wire	Data	?	Eliminates Utilities	
Wireless Chime Kit	Wireless	Data	Carlon	Eliminates Utilities	www.carlon.com

Appendix C: In-Depth Comparison of Various Production Systems

This section was originally included as an accompanying appendix to the Section 3 report on Functional Integration. It can stand alone as an interesting set of case studies across the housing industry and others.

Research Methods, Process and Sources

The Section 3 research method is based on a case study approach, although other methods are used. The case studies involve two building firms—Centex Homes and Bensonwood Homes. One observational study and two examples from the automobile industry and one from the computer industry were used as contrasting examples. Validation of the results to ensure generalization of the findings is achieved by the coherence between the cases, observations study, and system and communication theory.

Evidence Gathering
- Task 2 Literature Review
- VirginiaTech/Newport Team reports and discussion
- Bensonwood Homes site visit
- Centex Homes research and interview
- Tocci Builders interview
- Observation of a small condominium under construction
- Additional literature research
- GE Living Environments Home visit

Methods
- System and process analysis—task and transfer network approach
- System dynamics and life-cycle analysis—time and feedback loops
- Cause and effect analysis
- Pathway analysis—a multi-path history of development of Bensonwood Homes

Process
- Define conceptual frame—social, technical, economic
- Develop a system framework[1]
- Develop an 'essential' model utility system
- Develop an example or prototypical case
- Define the source and scope of system and component variability
- Discover root causes (five why's technique)

Data model of a utility

A data model of a utility system is composed of 3 elements: 1) generation or the production of the service (coal→electricity); 2) distribution or how the service is delivered (electricity is delivered by first a transmission grid and then again in a distribution grid); and 3) consumption, such as in lights for illuminating a home. Utilities themselves can be consumed to create other

---

[1] Hayek, HÄgerstrand, Kirschner, Fujimoto

utilities—gas is consumed to create hot water, electricity powers pumps that distribute the water to radiators (consumption). Diagrammatically this can be expressed as follows:

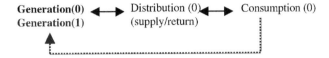

Figure 1: Data Model Of Utilities

The diagram is a data model, which shows entities and relationships. The model is not a flow model. The bottom arrow represents a recursive quality of the model meaning that a utility can serve another utility. This is important in modeling utility consumption in a home because electricity (a utility) is consumed by furnace producing heating for a home (a utility as well).

Relationships of Important Market and Industry Elements
Market and industry factors also affect the installation and use of utilities.
These factors can be geographically based and some can also be virtual. The following are some economic geography considerations:

- Material supply firms providing both new and existing building materials
- Distribution, logistics and transportation systems
- Appliance manufacturers providing new and replacements parts
- Repair and service supports and contracts, call centers
- Firms, organizations, professional societies
- Code, restrictions, standards (formal or informal)
- Skilled trades and unions, guilds, vocational schools
- Public housing agencies and other governmental entities
- Financial, legal, insurance and real-estate agencies
- Economic development agencies for both business and residential development

The importance of economic geographic factors is indirectly related to the entangled utility problem but is stall an important consideration. A new technology, whether it is a piece of hardware, software, process, tool or material can not be made immediately available to everyone everywhere at the same time. This is a kind of distribution problem most commonly seen in the telecommunication industry. New technology can be introduced quickly but new supporting infrastructure, including education and training, takes a significantly longer time to develop and put into practice.

Speculative Questions and Ideas
System descriptions of the home are problematic. Many attempts have been made to describe the house as a system. Various methods have been used but no general framework or common framework has emerged or has been seen as useful.

Is the variation in homes *situationally determined*—not determined by design? Do the various contexts, such as environmental, historical and regulatory, that homes are required to fit into dictate or determine variations?

If so, the design of homes will always require some effort to fit the home into the context and hence naturally limit the size and number of standard parts. For example, the number of small but standard parts for fitting and joining, standard sized materials and tools to cut and shape parts may be optimal?

Solution Opportunity Example #1—Manufacturing Best Practices

Numerous efforts by the housing industry have looked to see if practices in manufacturing could be useful in building homes. An entire market, though small, has developed around manufactured homes. These firms produce a small fraction of the total new homes built and do not address at all the home renovation industry. Despite many early attempts to develop a broader industrial process (e.g., Packaged House and Lustron homes in the late 1940s and early 1950s) no widespread industrial process has been developed similar to what has been achieved in automobile manufacturing.

Industrialization and manufacturing usually brings to mind automation, machines, Henry Ford, and the assembly line. Manufacturing, though, means more than automation. Manufacturing is also about people, organizations and tools. Toyota is by far the most efficient manufacturing operation in the world (ref. Spear, Fujimoto, Clark, Adler among others). The Toyota Production System (TPS) is not just the most efficient, it is also the most adaptable. TPS achieves its efficiency and effectiveness with one-half the level of automation employed by its competitors like GM and Ford.

Can TPS practices be useful in the home building industry?

Bensonwood Homes, one of our case study examples, surprisingly employs 21 of TPS's 30-documented best practices. These practices are employed not just in their shop, but also in their on-site work, engineering, design, and administration areas.

Bensonwood Case Study

Bensonwood Homes
- A defined building system of timber framing & panelized construction
- Uses a set of design rules (e.g., 2 by 2 grid)
- Has a process of continuous improvement with evolutionary learning capability

Key Practices Used By Bensonwood
- Defined balance between shop work vs. site work (quality of the *tools*)
- Shop work environment allows for effective *visualization* of the work
- Multi-skill/flexible tasks with supporting *physical layout*
- Stable employment
- Designed process steps and workstations
- Significant number of TPS practices especially 5, 16 and 17 (see Table 5)

These practices of Bensonwood led to some unintended consequences/side-affects that could be important to disentangling strategies. Meetings for planning the design and assembly of the frame afford the opportunity for everyone to hear the same things at the same time, which presents the opportunity to voice concerns and raise common issues. Cataloguing of designs for effective retrieval necessitated a strategy of modularization and design assembly, which allowed for easy reuse of past designs.

In order to effectively experiment with new ideas, such as disentangling utilities, a company must have: a system for accumulation of experience and knowledge, team participation over the course of a complete experimental cycle, multiple observers, reasonable control over system variables, and a method which involves in all aspects of the business. Bensonwood has these elements and has successfully been able to experiment and implement many improvements.

No.	Toyota[2]	Bensonwood Homes
1	Reduction of non-value added activities	√
2	Kanban—pull system (not zero inventory)	?
3	Levelization—product variety	√
4	Production plans based on dealer orders	√
5	Reduction of setup change time and lot size (priority over process time itself—information density)	√
6	Piece by piece transfer of parts	?
7	Flexible task assignment (multi-skill workforce)	√
8	Multi-task assignment	√
9	'U' shaped layout (first and last machines are side by side	√
10	Automatic detection of defects (but not automatic correction)	?
11	Fool-proof prevention of defects (e.g. specialized jigs)	√
12	Assembly line stop cord	N/A (speed consideration)
13	Andon cord (real-time feedback)	N/A
14	On-the-spot inspection by workers	√ (eye-sight accuracy)
15	Building in quality (doing things right the first time)	√ (timber frame joints)
16	Cleanliness, order and discipline (5-S)	√
17	Visual management	√
18	Frequent revision of SOPs	√
19	Quality Circles (problem solving teams)	√
20	Standard Tools for Quality Improvement	?
21	Worker Involvement in Preventive Maintenance	√
22	Low cost automation –just enough functions	√
23	Reduction of Process steps! (smaller number of workstation better defined units of production)***	√ (panel construction is optimized to material, tools, skills, person)
24	Stable employment of core workers ***	√
25	Long-term training of multi-skilled workers	√
26	Wage system based in part on skill accumulation	?
27	Internal promotion	√ (as practical)
28	Production supervisors as union workers	X
29	Cooperative relationship with labor unions	X
30	Communication and worker motivation	√

Table 1: A List Of TPS Practices That Bensonwood Homes Employs

Centex Homes Case Study

Centex Homes has realized that in their new developments it is important to build a prototype home and to analyze the construction process with all the relevant contractors involved. The prototype is more than a demonstration that shows that the new type of home can be built efficiently. The prototype is a kind of 'test fixture' or a platform to experiment, to ask "what if"

---

[2] From Takahiro Fujimoto

questions and to learn. The process of building the prototype is observable by all relevant parties and discussion about improvements takes place with all the key personnel present. The prototype is a method of visualization and experimentation. It should be noted that visualization and experimentation are at the roots of the over 50 years of success the Toyota production system has experienced.

Both Bensonwood Homes and Centex Homes have independently developed practices that resemble TPS best practices. These practices are not just for shop work or assembly line work but have application across the whole process of building homes.

These two case study examples suggest a closer look at TPS and other manufacturing best practices that may have wider applicability than previously thought.

Solution Opportunity Example #2—Information Exchange
During the course of this study the installation of utilities in a small condominium apartment was observed first hand. The apartment is situated in a building with some 20 other apartments and is small compared to a typical single family detached home (about 900 sq. ft.). Despite knowledge of the 15 strategies cited earlier to disentangle utilities they still got entangled. Can the apartment observation provide insight to the broader question? Yes. Future homes will need to incorporate a broader array of functionality and with increasingly sophisticated multi-layer assembled panelized construction, space and complexity will become limiting. The small apartment example with limited space for utilities mirrors the future problem.

So what happened? How do utilities get entangled?

Any home that is built:
- Has to fit the local context
- Decisions in related areas affect the outcome
- Not all information is in one place or held any one person
- Homes can not be completely specified before hand
- Not everything is available at the time & place decisions have to be made
- Comply with social, cultural and historical rules
- Comply with rules imposed by regulation and permits
- Comply with organizational rules and contracts
- Space and time limits

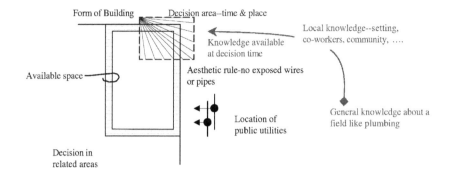

Figure 2: Effect of Location In Which Construction Actions Take Place

Ultimately, all actions are situated, meaning that they must take place in a specific place with specific constraints, which may be unaccounted for up until the action is actually happening. Plans often fail to be carried out exactly as designed because of unanticipated events but are clearly an important and vital preparation tool. One way to improve plans is to try to include more of the potential site based constraints during the planning process. In this sense places can be thought of as resources, which provide guiding information (ref. Suchman). However, it is generally not possible to have complete information during the planning phase.

The implications of this observation suggest that planning and design alone will not offer a complete solution. Support must be provided at the right time and place and within an appropriate time frame to those building a home.

Cell phones are becoming a necessary technology for coordination work. They, unfortunately, can create a condition of information overload. What if cell phones with cameras, annotation capability and task specific logistical support can be developed to better direct just the right information at the right time and place?

Corporate Descriptions of Home Builders
Three examples of Homebuilding Companies

Centex Homes
(Ref. http://www.centex.com/About_Centex/)

BACKGROUND

Established in 1950 in Dallas, Texas, today Centex Corporation is the nation's premier company in building and related services: Home Building, Home Services, Financial Services and Construction Services.

The company has approximately 17,000 employees located in more than 1,500 offices and construction job sites across the nation and in the U.K.

HOME BUILDING

Centex Homes builds and sells homes in approximately 560 neighborhoods serving more than 95 markets in 26 states.

Another Centex Home Building operation, Fox & Jacobs Homes, builds affordable housing that is value-engineered to be "the most home for your money." Centex also has other brand name builder subsidiaries across the nation: Wayne Homes builds on customer-owned lots; Centex Destination Properties specializes in resort and second homes; and CityHomes builds urban town homes in the Dallas market. Centex also has an international home building operation located in the United Kingdom, Fairclough Homes.

BUILDING SUPPLIES.

CTX Builders Supply, which sells construction supplies to both Centex and other conventional and manufactured home builders, operates in the Dallas/Fort Worth and Austin areas in Texas; Charlotte, NC and Phoenix, AZ.

HOME SERVICES

HomeTeam Pest Defense®, the nation's fourth largest residential pest management company, markets conventional pest management and termite treatment services. The company also offers two patented services, the Tubes in the Wall® pest control system and the Tubes Under the Slab® termite control system, that are installed during new home construction. HomeTeam also offers the Pest Defense® Termite Baiting System.

FINANCIAL SERVICES

CTX Mortgage Company, one of the nation's largest non-bank-affiliated retail mortgage originators, has more than 225 offices and is licensed to do business in 48 states.

Centex Home Equity Company offers non-conforming mortgages and home equity loans directly to borrowers and indirectly through mortgage brokers. The company has over 130 office locations and is licensed to do business in 47 states.

Centex's Title and Insurance operations provide nationwide residential and commercial title insurance and settlement services, including low-cost property reports and appraisal products. Centex has more than 80 title and insurance offices and is licensed to do business across the nation. Centex also offers homeowners' insurance as well as auto, boat, commercial, home warranty and umbrella policies.

Bensonwood
http://www.bensonwood.com/press/cohistory.html

BACKGROUND

Through process and product, improving people's lives. This is the essential statement of the company's mission. The product began in 1974 with Tedd Benson's early efforts to revive the craft of timber framing. Tedd found in the historic buildings of New England a legacy of durable, honestly crafted buildings, the heart of which were framed in heavy timbers joined by traditional mortise and tenon joinery. Many of these structures had stood for 200 or more years, and were still strong as long as their roofs had been maintained. He also found that the knowledge of this form of construction was virtually forgotten by modern practitioners of wood framing, who, in the pursuit of ever faster and cheaper ways of assembling the structure of buildings, had lost this valuable craft. He began by studying old barns and houses in New England, and then built his first few frames using the historical joinery he had observed in those buildings. He began to attract dedicated woodworkers to the hill country of southwestern New Hampshire. Together they saw that their task was to rediscover long-forgotten hand framing techniques and integrate them with modern tools and sensibilities. The goal was to create authentic, durable, yet modern, frames; thus they pursued a process that enriched the workers and created a product that thrilled clients.

THE COMPANY

The company is composed of over 50 team members, about half of which are crafts persons working with timbers, and the other half are involved with design, project management, or office support. On staff are: Dr. Ben Brungraber, Ph.D., P.E., one of the most recognized timber engineers in the country, two structural engineers, two registered architects, one architect intern, six designers, three CAD specialists, three project managers, and a number of master timber framers with over 12 years experience. BWC also often has visiting artisans from foreign countries, such as temple carpenters from Japan, French compaignons, or timber craftsmen (journeyman) trained in the European guild tradition. The staff constantly enriches their craft from these associations. Benson Woodworking has been active in the Timber Framer's Guild of North America since its inception in 1984, with Tedd Benson as a founding member. The current Executive Director of the Guild is Joel McCarty, a former longtime employee of BWC. In 1995, Benson Woodworking became a charter member of the Timber Frame Business Council.

BENSONWOOD HOMES AND OPEN-BUILT

In the late 1990s, BWC decided to create a new division of the company, Bensonwood Homes. The goals are: 1) to provide whole house packages of pre-engineered volume frames based on Open-Built principles; 2) reduce costs of the frame/enclosure package by advancements in design and production technology; 3) improve the speed of delivery around the country by increased team participation with the area associate network.

Appendix D: Workshop Results

A workshop was held at TIAX in May, 2004, at which the TIAX/MIT research team attempted to frame the problem of disentangling for discussion with a small group of building industry professionals. The breadth of the discussion that ensued underscores the difficulty in attempting to decouple entangled utilities from other problems facing the building industry today. While there was disagreement on some counts, the following list of concerns were highlighted when workshop participants were asked for input as to what should be done next to solve the problem of entangled utilities. The workshop allowed our team to solicit critical review of our theories and at the same time gain additional insights into potential solution strategies that may have been overlooked.

- A new business model must be created to capture the lifetime value of disentangling.
- A building code written to ensure houses work for 100 years (or 30 years) would require higher standards, one of which would have to be disentangling solutions, which would allow utility repair and renovation over the 100 years.
- An adaptable (disentangled) home would provide less risk to an insurer. HUD could take advantage of this in FHA homes.
- A builder who provided a repair and renovation over the life of the homes they build would have incentive to disentangle.
- The current subcontracting system is an impediment to innovation, cost prediction, and quality control.
- Work currently performed by subcontractors could be reduced by creating factory manufactured components and systems that require less assembly labor.
- Absorbing subcontractors into builders as assemblers or integrators may allow greater control of innovation, cost, and quality.
- One-off, factory made homes may offer the best opportunity for capturing the value created during initial construction by disentangling (Pulte, Centex, etc. should be "written off," because they will not be able to capture the value of disentangling).
- A replicatable prototype home and process should be completed by 2006 to demonstrate and test the following ideas.
- Integrate subcontractors into suppliers and builders (as they have been in other industries i.e. automobile).
- Components with standard connections and quick assembly (3D grid) (An international consortium could be created to develop standards).
- Adaptability over time (renovation should be tried & cost quantified).
- A computer system which allows faster design as well as better supply chain management and information distribution throughout the building process and beyond and thus disentangling.
- Kitchens (Merrilat) are a great example of standardization, automation, and innovation.
- The real problem is "disembedding" or "disemboweling" of utilities, separating them from the more permanent building structure.
- Economic analysis should be conducted to determine why the industry has developed to our current state. Why does Pulte (a successful company) operate they way they do?

Additional References

Akrich, Madeleine, "The De-scription of Technical Objects" in Wiebe E. Bijker and John Law, "Shaping Technology/Buildinig Society—Studies in Sociotechnical Change", MIT Press, Cambridge MA, 1997

Ball, Michael, *"Chasing a Snail: Innovation and Housebuilding Firms' Strategies"*, Housing *Studies*, Vol 14, No. 1. 9-22, 1999

Barlow, James and Michael Ball, *"Introduction—Improving British Housing Supply"*, Housing Studies, Vol. 14, No. 1, 5-8, 1999

Barlow, James, *"From Craft Production to Mass Customization—Innovation Requirements for the UK Housebuilding Industry"*, Housing Studies, Vol. 14, No. 1 23-42, 1999

Baldwin, Cariss Y, Kim B. Cark, *"Design Rules—Vol. 1 The Power of Modularity"*, The MIT Press, Cambridge, MA 2000

Baldwin, Cariss Y, Kim B. Cark, *"Where Do Transactions Come From?"* from authors, 2003

Clark, Kim and Takahiro Fujimoto, *"The Process of Product Development"*, in Product Development Performance, Harvard Business School Press, Boston, MA, 1991

Cowan, Ruth Schwartz, *"The Consumption Junction: A proposal for research Strategies in the Sociology of Technology"* in Wiebe E. Bijker, Thomas P. Hughes, and Trevor J. Pinch, ed. "The Social Construction of Technological System", The MIT Press, Cambridge, MA 1999

Eppinger, Steven D., *"Innovation at the Speed of Information"*, Harvard Business Review, January 2001

Fujimoto, Takahiro, "The Evolution of a Manufacturing System at Toyota", Oxford University Press, New York, NY, 1999

Gleick, James, *"When the House Starts Talking to Itself"*, New York Times, November 16, 2003

Kukla, Charles, Elizabeth Clemens, *"The Ethnographic Approach to Product Development"*, in T. Horgan, M.L. Joroff, W.L. Porter and D. Schön, *Excellence by Design: Transforming Workplace and Work Practice*, John Wiley & Sons, 1999

Kukla, Charles, Elizabeth Clemens, Robert Morse, Deborah Cash, *Designing Effective Systems: A Tool Approach, in Usability: Turning Technology into Tools*, ed. Paul S. Adler, Terry Winograd, Oxford University Press, New York, NY 1992

Kukla, Charles, Turid Horgan, *"The Synthesis of Ideas and Practices: The LX Workplace Experiment"*, in T. Horgan, M.L. Joroff, W.L. Porter and D. Schön, Excellence *by Design: Transforming Workplace and Work Practice*, John Wiley & Sons, 1999

Joroff, Michael L., William L. Porter, Barbara Feinberg, Charles Kukla, *"The agile workplace"*, Journal of Corporate Real Estate, Vol. 5, No. 4, , pp. 293-311 September 2003

Mackay, W.E., *"Is Paper Safer? The Role of Paper Flight Strips in Air Traffic Control"*, ACM/Transactions on Computer-Human Interaction. Vol. 6, pp. 311-340, 2000

O'Brien, Michael, *"A Brief History of System Additions and Material Innovation in the Light Frame House"*, Virginia Tech, from author

Takahiro Fujimoto, *The Evolution of a Manufacturing System at Toyota*, Oxford University Press, New York, NY, 1999

Thomke , Stefan H., *Experimentation Matters: Unlocking the Potential of New Technologies for Innovation*; Harvard Business School Press, 2003

Thomke, Stefan, "Enlightened Experimentation—The New Imperative for Innovation, Harvard Business Review, February 2001

Thomke, Stefan and Rick von Hipper, *"Customers as Innovators—A New Way to Create Value"*, Harvard Business Review, April 2002

Wakefield, Ron, Michael O'Brien, "*A Preliminary Method for Evaluating Physical Design Characteristics and Whole House Performance Scoring*", from authors

Warde, Alan, Elizabeth Shove, Dale Southerton, " Convenience, schedules and sustainability", Lancaster University, draft paper for ESF workshop- on sustainable consumption, March 27-29, 1998

Zuboff, Shoshana and James Maxmin *"The Support Economy: Why Corporations Are Failing Individuals and the Next Episode of Capitalism"* Penguin Press, USA, 2004

Path Technology Roadmap: Whole House and Building Process Redesign, Year One Progress Report

Rethinking Construction—The Report of the Construction Task Force, Department of Trade and Industry, London, UK 1998

Lightning Source UK Ltd.
Milton Keynes UK
UKHW050648221121
394386UK00005B/129